# STRATEGIES FOR TEACHING AND LEARNING PROFESSIONAL LIBRARY

## Creating Your Classroom
# Community

LOIS BRIDGES

 Stenhouse Publishers

 The Galef Institute

**Strategies for Teaching and Learning** Professional Library

*Administrators: Supporting School Change* by Robert Wortman
*Assessment: Continuous Learning* by Lois Bridges
*Creating Your Classroom Community* by Lois Bridges
*Drama as a Way of Knowing* by Paul G. Heller
*Math as a Way of Knowing* by Susan Ohanian
*Music as a Way of Knowing* by Nick Page

Look for announcements of future titles in this series on dance, second language learners, literature, physical education, science, visual arts, and writing.

Stenhouse Publishers, 431 York Street, York, Maine 03909
The Galef Institute, 11050 Santa Monica Boulevard, Third Floor, Los Angeles, California 90025

Copyright © 1995 The Galef Institute.

*Library of Congress Cataloging-in-Publication Data*
Bridges, Lois
        Creating your classroom community / Lois Bridges.
            p.     cm. — (Strategies for teaching and learning professional library)
        Includes bibliographical references (p.  ).
        ISBN 1-57110-049-0 (alk. paper)
            1. Teaching—Handbooks, manuals, etc.   2. Learning—Handbooks, manuals, etc.   3. Classroom
        environment—Handbooks, manuals, etc.   4. Teacher-student relationships—Handbooks, manuals, etc.
        I. Title   II. Series.
        LB1025.3.B57   1995
        371.1'02—dc20                                                                                      96-45750
                                                                                                                 CIP

Manufactured in the United States of America on acid-free paper
01 00 99 98 97 96 8 7 6 5 4 3 2 1

Dear Colleague,

This is an exciting time for us to be educators.

Research across disciplines informs our understanding of human learning and development. We know how to support students as active, engaged learners in our classrooms. We know how to continuously assess student learning and development to make sensitive, instructional decisions. This is the art of teaching—knowing how to respond effectively at any given moment to our students' developmental needs.

As educators, we know that learning the art of teaching takes time, practice, and lots of professional support. To that end, the Strategies for Teaching and Learning Professional Library was developed. Each book invites you to explore theory (to know why) in the context of exciting teaching strategies (to know how) connected to evaluation of your students' learning as well as your own (to know you know). In addition, you'll find in-depth information about the unique rigors and challenges of each discipline, to help you make the most of the rich learning and teaching opportunities each discipline offers.

Use the books' *Dialogues* on your own and in the study groups to reflect upon your practices. The Dialogues invite responses to self-evaluative questions, experimentation with new instructional strategies in classrooms, and perhaps a rethinking of learning philosophy and classroom practices stimulated by new knowledge and understanding.

*Shoptalks* offer you lively reviews of the best and latest professional literature including professional journals and associations.

*Teacher-To-Teacher Field Notes* are full of tips and experiences from practicing educators who offer different ways of thinking about teaching practices and a wide range of classroom strategies they've found practical and successful.

As you explore and reflect on teaching and learning, we believe you'll continue to refine and extend your teaching art, and enjoy your professional life and the learning lives of your students.

Here's to the art of teaching!

Lois Bridges
Professional Development Editorial Director,
The Galef Institute

The Strategies for Teaching and Learning Professional Library is part of the Galef Institute's school reform initiative *Different Ways of Knowing*.

*Different Ways of Knowing* is a philosophy of education based on research in child development, cognitive theory, and multiple intelligences. It offers teachers, administrators, specialists, and other school and district educators continuing professional growth opportunities integrated with teaching and learning materials. The materials are supportive of culturally and linguistically diverse school populations and help all teachers and children to be successful. Teaching strategies focus on interdisciplinary, thematic instruction integrating history and social studies with the performing and visual arts, literature, writing, math, and science. Developed with the leadership of Senior Author Linda Adelman, *Different Ways of Knowing* has been field tested in hundreds of classrooms across the country.

For more information, write or call

**The Galef Institute**
11050 Santa Monica Boulevard, Third Floor, Los Angeles, California 90025
Tel 310.479.8883
Fax 310.473.9720


**Strategies for Teaching and Learning** Professional Library

**Contributors**

*President*
Linda Adelman

*Vice President Programs and Communications*
Sue Beauregard

*Professional Development Editorial Director*
Lois Bridges

*Editor*
Resa Gabe Nikol

*Editorial Assistants*
Elizabeth Finison, Wendy Sallin

*Designers*
Melvin Harris, Delfina Marquez-Noé, Sarah McCormick, Jennifer Swan Myers, Julie Suh

*Photographers*
Ted Beauregard, Dana Ross


*Twenty-one teachers opened the doors of their classrooms, invited me in, and enabled me to share their ideas and insights within the pages of this text. I am most grateful to them all. Thanks also to Judy DeWitt and Karolynne Gee.*
                                                                                    —LB

Pam Adair
Martha Ahlman
Judy Bloomington-Vinke
Chris Boyd
Greg Chapnick
Kittye Copeland
Alice Dalzell

Cathy Howard
Beth Huntzinger
Mary Kitagawa
Bonnie Laster
Rena Malkofsky
Leslie Mangiola
Deborah Manning

Janice Marshall
Vera Milz
Nan Mohr
Denise Ogren
Barbara Poro
Susan Raedeke
Peggy Smullin

*Special thanks to Andrew G. Galef and Bronya Pereira Galef for their continuing commitment to our nation's children and educators.*

# Contents

*Chapter 1*
# What Is Community?

What is *community?* My *Webster's* offers this definition: *The condition of living with others; friendly association; fellowship.* Teachers and students alike need as much friendly association and fellowship as possible. Happily there are ways, specific strategies that we can use, to create the mutual sharing and caring that characterize true fellowship and friendly communities. In this book, you'll discover ways to make classroom hours count for both you and your students. Individually and together, you'll derive a new understanding of yourselves as capable, creative learners who enjoy learning and living together as members of a classroom community.

Let's begin with your positive beliefs about learning and teaching. The collaborative, community-building strategies you'll learn in this book assume that 1) you really like children; 2) you believe that all children are capable, creative learners; 3) you enjoy learning yourself; 4) you enjoy teaching. With those beliefs in place, the strategies will make sense to you and will work.

What we personally believe about learning and teaching helps us create a thriving classroom community. But we also need to understand the scientific knowledge regarding learning and teaching. Educators now possess more than thirty years of research across disciplines. They know what learning is and how best to support it in classrooms. This scientific knowledge is known as generative-constructivist learning theory.

Generative-constructivist learning theory isn't the easiest name to remember—or even to say—but it's easily understood as eight overarching principles.

## What We Know About Learning

**Learners learn what matters to them.** The most significant learning—and often the most effortless—arises from that which arouses the interest and meets the needs of the learner. Therefore, students must have some choice about what and how they will learn.

**Learners construct meaning for themselves.** The most significant and enduring learning is constructed by the learner, not imposed from without. Students learn best when they are actively engaged in planning, monitoring, and controlling their own learning.

**Learners thrive in a safe, supportive environment.** Learners must be confident that they are safe from negative repercussions. We begin with our children's strengths, celebrating all that they can do, encouraging them to build from there.

**Learners use multiple intelligences to learn at their own developmental pace.** Learners have access to multiple modalities to explore, refine, and extend their learning at their own developmental pace. Traditionally, we have favored language as the medium of thought and learning in school. Howard Gardner (1983) reminds us that there are other modalities that for many persons are comfortable and accessible avenues of exploration and expression. An effective curriculum develops the multiple intelligences of children—their artistic and social strategies as well as verbal and math strategies, intuitive as well as logical thinking.

### SHOPTALK

Gardner, Howard. *Frames of Mind: The Theory of Multiple Intelligences*. New York: Basic Books, 1983.

Gardner effectively unlaces the straitjacket of psychometric theory and information processing that has tightly bound our view of the human mind. What emerges is a new understanding of the mind as an infinitely complex and subtle, multi-dimensional tool. Gardner argues that human beings possess at least seven intelligences which have largely been ignored in schools. The ramifications are clear. When children can explore their understandings across multiple intelligences, the curriculum becomes more meaningful and accessible to all.

## SHOPTALK

Goodman, Kenneth. *What's Whole in Whole Language?* Portsmouth, New Hampshire: Heinemann, 1986.

Unofficially recognized as the whole language "bible," this is a slim book with a mighty message. More than 300,000 copies have sold, and it's now available in Spanish, French, and Japanese. Teachers, parents, and administrators relate to the straightforward manner in which Goodman sets forth the principles of whole language or learner-centered teaching and learning. As he explains, whole language is both scientific (founded on more than 30 years of interdisciplinary research) and humanistic (trusting, respectful, and caring toward the learner). The same may be said for this indispensable book.

**Learners use subjects and skills as tools to learn about a topic.** A learner-centered classroom involves rich, cross-disciplinary research that focuses on a theme or big idea. It is in the service of exploring a theme that students develop the intellectual tools that will serve them a lifetime.

**Learners use the world as their laboratory.** Students shouldn't be confined to the four walls of the classroom. As they work to find answers to their questions, they explore resources outside the classroom and invite outside experts in to share information. In this way, students learn that it's possible to gather information from primary sources—other human beings.

**Learners explore their learning over multiple drafts.** Teachers who understand constructivist learning theory encourage rough draft thinking and communicating. Children are invited to explore, refine, and elaborate their meaning over multiple drafts and to express their evolving understandings through a variety of presentational formats that include art, dance, drama, and music as well as oral and written language.

**Learners never stop learning.** One line of inquiry leads to another. The measure of true learning is not recall of old material, but new questions that address new possibilities, leading the learner into new realms of exploration. So once we've completed a unit of study with our students, we not only ask them, "What did you learn?" but we also ask, "What will you learn next?"

We can represent the eight principles of generative-constructivist learning theory as a chart that contrasts a traditional, teacher-centered philosophy of education with a learner-centered one.

| Teacher-Centered | Learner-Centered |
|---|---|
| Teacher controls and directs learning | Teacher nurtures and facilitates learning |
| Step-ladder model: learning progresses from simple to complex; part to whole | Kaleidoscope model: whole learning pattern shifts and changes as new knowledge and experiences are assimilated |
| Accuracy is valued; mistakes must be avoided | Risk-taking is essential to learning; "mistakes" are a necessary outcome of learning |
| Learners must master what is taught, when it is taught; all students experience some degree of failure | Learners develop at their own pace; learning experiences help everyone succeed |
| Learning represents the ability to reproduce or recall teacher-taught material | Learning represents the ability to use new understanding in novel ways; to generate new questions which lead to further learning and more questions |

*What you believe about the purpose of education and your role in shaping your students' educational experiences influences how you interact with your students, the curriculum you create, and how and what you evaluate.*

As a student in the teacher credential program at the University of California in Riverside, California, I was required to write my philosophy of education before I could graduate. It wasn't an easy task. But it was an invaluable learning experience, and, ultimately, proved a most helpful teaching tool. Your educational philosophy pervades your curriculum and directs every step you take in your classroom. With an examined philosophy, you are likely to get where you want to go. Without one, proceed with caution! What you believe about the purpose of education and your role in shaping your students' educational experiences influences how you interact with your students, the curriculum you create, and how and what you evaluate.

At Fair Oaks School in Redwood City, California, teachers write Visitor's Guides to their classrooms. The Guides provide a succinct statement of each teacher's educational philosophy as well as a description of the activities a visitor to the classroom can expect to see and why. The Guides are kept in an envelope next to the door so that every visitor who steps inside the classroom can, at a glance, share in the teacher's instructional vision and interpret the wide range of teaching and learning interactions occurring in the room.

Karen Smith, former sixth-grade teacher at Laurel School, in the inner city of Phoenix, Arizona, set these goals for herself and her students:

- Encourage students to think and take pleasure in using their intellects.
- Help students learn to get along with and appreciate others.
- Manage the day-to-day environment smoothly so other goals can be accomplished.
- Encourage students to be self-reliant and sure of themselves.

Bobbi Fisher, kindergarten teacher at Josiah Haynes School in Sudbury, Massachusetts, and the author of *Joyful Learning: A Whole Language Kindergarten* (1991) outlines her beliefs about learning:

- Children learn naturally.
- Children know a lot about literacy before kindergarten.
- All children can learn.
- Children learn best when learning is kept whole, meaningful, interesting, and functional.
- Children learn best as a community of learners in a non-competitive environment.
- Children learn best by talking and doing in a social context.

## SHOPTALK

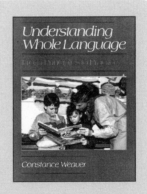

Weaver, Constance. *Understanding Whole Language: From Principles to Practice.* Portsmouth, New Hampshire: Heinemann, 1990.

Constance Weaver has done it again. Like her *Reading Process to Practice* (1988), her latest offering is a treasure-trove of both theoretical and practical information. This aptly named book explains the whole of whole language (also known as "learner-centered" or "generative-constructivist"): what it is and isn't; how it has evolved over time; what research has to say in support of it; how whole language teachers handle phonics, skills, and assessment; and how to implement whole language in your classroom and school. Especially helpful to those new to whole language are several starter bibliographies on whole language theory and practice, assessment, developmental spelling, and classroom reading, writing, and literacy. And a chapter by Diane Stephens, "What Does the Research Say? Research in Support of Whole to Part," provides information to administrators and parents.

# DIALOGUE

What are my assumptions about teaching? What am I trying to accomplish? What do I believe about

- the purpose of education?

  _____

  _____

- my role as a teacher?

  _____

  _____

- my students' roles as learners?

  _____

  _____

- the meaning of curriculum—how would I define curriculum?

  _____

  _____

- the role of evaluation?

  _____

  _____

How might I represent my philosophy?

- ☐ as a list of educational goals
- ☐ as a chart contrasting different models of education
- ☐ as a creative representation—narrative, poem, song, letter to my students' parents, photographic essay, Visitor's Guide to my classroom
- ☐ as visual symbols.

## S H O P T A L K

Fisher, Bobbi. *Joyful Learning: A Whole Language Kindergarten*. Portsmouth, New Hampshire: Heinemann, 1991.

Imagine spending a day working side by side with veteran kindergarten teacher Bobbi Fisher in her classroom! You'd learn how she effectively organizes her classroom for active learning and how she schedules for optimum learning. You'd also discover practical approaches to dramatic play, math manipulatives, shared reading, and the like. If you can't travel to Sudbury, Massachusetts, where Bobbi teaches at the Josiah Haynes School, then read her book—and reap the benefits of her expertise and practical know-how.

Watson, Dorothy, Carolyn Burke and Jerome Harste. *Whole Language: Inquiring Voices*. New York: Scholastic, 1989.

What does it mean to be a learner-centered teacher? This delightful book answers the question through thought-provoking commentary, deft descriptions of teachers and students involved in classroom inquiry, and challenging invitations to the reader to engage in professional self-evaluation. The slim, easy-to-read volume captures the excitement teachers feel when they shed the restrictive role of teacher-as-imparter-of-information and emerge as teacher-as-inquirer. They enjoy the freedom to listen to and learn from their own intuition, to employ their theoretical understandings of language and learning in their teaching, and to collaborate with colleagues and their students.

Moving from a teacher-centered classroom to a learner-centered one requires time, patience, and self-reflection, but those who have made the change testify to the benefits for both themselves and their students. Kittye Copeland, who teaches in a multiage classroom in Columbia, Missouri, explains the positive changes in her classroom once she freed herself from textbooks and began to view herself as a co-learner with her students: "When my curriculum was textbook-driven, I couldn't get to each child as a whole person.

My students were receivers of my information, not active, responsible, individual learners. When I moved from a teacher giving information to a teacher engaged in my own reading, writing, and learning, it enabled students to become engaged themselves. When children encounter teachers who see themselves as real writers, readers, and learners instead of only instructors, they discover the benefits of education—and no gold stars are needed."

*Chapter 2*

# Make Yourself at Home

There's a lot about my own schooling I don't remember, but I do remember Mrs. Lutz, my kindergarten teacher. Forever smiling in my memory, I see her standing at the classroom door, greeting us by name as we arrived. And at the end of our short school day, she stood by the door once again, embracing us or shaking our hands good-bye, sending every one of us on our way with a personal comment or note of praise. I loved Mrs. Lutz and I loved kindergarten.

Thirty-some years later, as a teacher myself, I realize that it was no accident that I loved Mrs. Lutz and our kindergarten class. Her post by the door as we entered and left the classroom helped us know that she cared about each one of us. As she looked me in the eye, squeezed my hand, and said, "Good-bye, Lois, I'll see you tomorrow!" I knew that she recognized and liked me as an individual. Her look, words, and touch bound each child to her and she to them. Interpersonal relationships—a sense of caring and sharing—is not peripheral to effective classrooms, it's basic. "Community in itself," writes Ralph Peterson in his book *Life in a Crowded Place: Making a Learning Community* (1992), "is more important to learning than any method or technique."

For that reason, primary teacher Chris Boyd works to make contact with each one of her students individually at the beginning of every day either through eye contact, a hug, or verbally. "I treat each child differently depending on what's best for the child," Boyd, who teaches at Roadrunner

School in Phoenix, Arizona, explains. "Some children need immediate physical contact to start each day, some need to be left alone and just acknowledged, others need a plan such as a place to sit or thing to do."

### *Getting To Know You*

Communities grow from individuals. To create a strong community, we must know the individuals that make up that community. Our first order of business, then, as sensitive, caring teachers is to get to know our students; to discover each one as a unique individual with special interests, abilities, and needs. We become acquainted with our students in much the same way we do with our friends outside the classroom; we talk with them, invite them to talk about themselves, and listen and respond.

By reaching out to our students in a personal way, we accomplish two important goals. First, children feel valued as individuals. Realizing that we want to know them as real people helps children feel good about themselves psychologically, socially, and academically. It tells children that we know them, care for them, and want to learn with and from them. That's empowering!

Secondly, once we understand our students' interests, abilities, and needs, we can use that information in planning our curriculum and instruction. In this way, we can involve students in learning experiences that matter to them. We begin with their needs and interests and build from there. By using our students as "curricular informants" (Harste 1984), we can with confidence, on any given school day, recommend a book that we know will make a difference for a student, suggest a topic for a research project that will excite another, and provide still another student with just the right supplies needed for expression through visual art. The most effective teaching is responsive. "The essence of the teacher's art," writes Margaret Donaldson, author of *Children's Minds* (1978), "lies in deciding what help is needed…in any given instance and how this help may best be offered." When we really know and understand our students, we can offer help that moves them forward.

There are many ways to get to know our students. Here are some of my favorites.

**Getting-to-know-you questionnaires.** Judy Bloomingdale-Vinke, a language arts resource teacher for Lawndale School District in California, finds a simple interview is an easy yet effective way to gain insight into her students' interests, abilities, and needs. At the beginning of the school year, she arranges her schedule so she can pull individual students aside for the interview. If finding time to conduct formal interviews seems overwhelming, try these alternatives: invite students to interview each other and present their findings to the whole class; ask older students in to interview younger students; or send the questionnaire home and ask parents to complete it with their kids. Certainly, older students can write answers themselves. The interviews can be audiotaped or videotaped and shared with the whole class. Students might enjoy writing and answering their own questions, too. Bloomingdale-Vinke finds the exchange with each student so helpful that she won't give up conducting the interviews herself.

**Getting To Know You**

My name is _____

_____

My birthday is _____

_____

Something I could teach someone is _____

_____

A way I'm different and unique from someone else is _____

_____

The world would be a better place if _____

_____

I like it when _____

_____

I've learned a lot about _____

_____

A good book I've read is _____

_____

I liked the book because _____

_____

A holiday I like is _____

_____

Some of my favorite things include _____

_____

A time I remember best is _____

_____

It's important to _____

_____

I'd like to tell my teacher or ask my teacher _____

_____

```
DIALOGUE

What do I do to get to know my students?

_____

_____

_____

_____
```

*Establishing an open dialogue with parents creates an educational partnership.*

Cathy Howard at Ohlone School in Palo Alto, California, gathers similar information from a questionnaire she sends parents the first week of school. "Getting To Know Your Child" helps Howard understand her students and their home experiences. She also learns about parents' expectations for their children's education. Her letter and questionnaire establish an open dialogue with parents and an educational partnership that lasts throughout the year.

### Getting To Know Your Child

*Dear Parents:*

*This information is most helpful to me as I get to know your child and you. Please send it to me at your earliest convenience. Thank you.*

- *What changes (health, maturity, interests) have occurred in the life of your child this summer?*

- *What areas of school life has your child especially enjoyed?*

- *Toward what areas of school life has your child expressed negative or ambivalent feelings?*

- *In general, how is your child's self-concept? Does he or she believe in his or her abilities?*

- *What special needs (academic, social, personal) does your child have?*

- *What goals do you have for your child this year?*

- *Where does your child go after school?*

- *What are favorite afterschool or weekend interests and activities?*

- *What else do you want me to know about your child or about you?*

*From_____ Date_____*

*The Whole Language Catalog: Forms for Authentic Assessment* © 1994 edited by Lois Bridges Bird, Kenneth S. Goodman and Yetta M. Goodman

**Artifact boxes.** Nan Mohr, a fifth-grade teacher at Shuey Elementary School in Rosemead, California, devotes the first month of school to helping her class get acquainted. She and her fifth graders sit in a circle every morning and discuss personal topics such as their favorite books, or afterschool activities. Mohr also invites them to explore a range of modalities as they share. They draw the important events of their lives on timelines or storyboards; they create "name art," abstract representations of their written names; and design coats of arms, in which they depict their families, homes, and personal likes and dislikes. Mohr makes time to post and discuss each creation. She also asks her students to present their talents and hobbies. Students read poetry, make models, sketch portraits, play musical instruments, and dance for their classmates.

Artifact boxes stand out as Mohr's favorite way to have students get to know themselves and each other better. Students bring shoeboxes from home along with items that represent themselves. Each artifact tells a personal story or reveals a family history. Students bring favorite books, beloved stuffed animals, bowling trophies, winning team soccer shirts, birthstones, and personal treasures of all sorts. "We come to know personal preferences," Mohr reports, "and students experience acceptance of their uniqueness and receive recognition."

**Personal history posters.** Teacher Chris Boyd, in Phoenix, Arizona, offers yet another way to get acquainted with students. She sends home a letter and asks parents to help their children create a visual history of their family. Each child takes home a sheet of tagboard. With their parents' help, they spend several weeks gluing on the tagboard family photographs of their home, vacations, and other family members and friends. They also draw their family tree, photocopy birth certificates, and list favorite books and activities. Boyd takes pictures of children without family photos and encourages foster parents to cut and paste pictures from magazines showing what their foster child likes and has experienced. "Then the fun begins," Boyd reports. On the day

the posters are due, "the children spend the morning sharing each other's lives. But they also get the posters out of their special place all during the year just to look at them with their friends or to share them with an older helper, parent, or any classroom visitor."

---

**Personal History Posters**

*Dear Parents:*

*We are now beginning a study of the concept of history. We will be exploring the early history of our country and various other events and phenomena that affect our lives. As a major part of this study, the children will have a chance to look at their own histories. Today we are sending home a sheet of tagboard with your child's name at the top. As you discuss with your child past events in your family's history, record as much information as you can on the sheet. The idea is to make a visual history of your child or family. These posters can be decorated front and back. They will be laminated and put into a giant class scrapbook to be displayed during our Thanksgiving Feast. The book will remain in the classroom and the pages will be sent home at the end of the year.*

*Suggestions*

- *use photos, drawings, cut-out magazine pictures, and so on*
- *label baby pictures of your child or other family members*
- *draw your family tree*
- *make maps of where family members were born*
- *make copies of birth announcements or other certificates*
- *include names of favorite books, poems, games, or songs*
- *include significant dates for your family or child*
- *make copies of footprints and handprints (past or present)*
- *include names, pictures, or postcards of family vacation places*
- *include leaves from a backyard tree or pressed flowers*
- *make pictures or drawings of favorite pets*
- *include wish drawings (what your child wants to do)*
- *include pictures or drawings of favorite toys, of significant people in your child's life, or of other favorites such as food or restaurants*
- *be creative and have fun! Learn and remember together!*

*Please don't put anything on the poster that you don't want laminated, or that is thick (it won't go through the machine). Please don't use staples; use glue and tape only.*

*Historically yours,*
*Chris Boyd*

**Dialogue journals.** Of course, there's no substitute for conversation. Chit-chat about the small details of our daily lives builds intimacy between friends—and between teachers and students. Often, there's not enough time in a busy school day to talk informally with every student. For that reason, some teachers like Mary Kitagawa, fifth-sixth grade teacher at Marks Meadow School in Amherst, Massachusetts, rely on written conversations with students in dialogue journals. Her students may write about anything on their minds. Kitagawa responds, asking questions, commenting on their thoughts and feelings, and interacting with them in writing in much the same way she would verbally. "It makes for powerful interactions," explains Kitagawa, "and I see the kids develop not only as writers but also as people. It also provides me with a vehicle for interpersonal dynamics with individuals that is not always possible in the competition for attention that occurs all day in the classroom." It can be time-consuming. Kitagawa often responds to journals at home in the evening. She doesn't object. "The benefits are worth the extra effort."

*Chit-chat about the small details of our daily lives builds intimacy between friends—and between teachers and students.*

---

### DIALOGUE

What new ideas might I try to get to know my students?

_____

_____

_____

_____

---

## Rituals and Ceremonies

Rituals and ceremonies are a part of everything we do; from the way we roll out of bed and begin a new day, to the way we enter matrimony and begin a new life. Not surprisingly, rituals and ceremonies are part of classroom life as well. The beginning and ending of a school day are often ritualized. We find ritual in the way students gather on the rug for a story, and in the positions and attitudes students assume as they begin a writer's workshop. You can consciously use classroom ritual and ceremony to create and shape community. In *Life in a Crowded Place* (1992), Ralph Peterson describes the potential and power of classroom ceremony: "It forms attitudes and creates a feeling of group purpose. It can fire emotions, affect a contemplative mood, and foster or bring about an internal order...It is a powerful tool to help us center the group and turn attention to the events that are to follow."

*Field Notes: Teacher-To-Teacher*

When we take attendance, we always say we miss each person that is absent and wish they were at school. When a child returns from being out of school, I always say I'm glad they are back and that we missed them.

*Chris Boyd
Roadrunner School
Phoenix, Arizona*

*Ritualized opening ceremonies surround the children with a comfortable, predictable sequence of events which both welcome and reassure them.*

**Beginning the day.** Beginnings are always significant. Teachers usually pay a lot of attention to the beginning of the school day because they know it often sets the tone for the entire day. Indeed, if an unexpected fire drill or school assembly cancels the opening ceremony, the rest of the day just doesn't seem to fall into place. Ritualized opening ceremonies surround the children with a comfortable, predictable sequence of events which both welcome and reassure them: "I belong here. This is my classroom where I am valued and respected as a learner."

Such ceremonies need not be elaborate. In Palo Alto, California, Lisa Dhollande and Sara Hammond invite their kindergartners to begin their day on the rug with a book they choose from baskets brimming with beautiful children's literature. Parents are welcome to gather children on their laps and read aloud. This cozy ten-minute sharing of books helps center children and gently ease them into a new school day.

Janice Marshall, a kindergarten teacher at Keeling School in Tucson, Arizona, opens her classroom door ten minutes early and invites the children to come in at their leisure. That way she has the opportunity to talk with each child. She gives the children a 20-minute settling-in time. They have a chance to visit with Marshall and each other, share objects brought from home, sign the attendance sheet, and, in general, acclimate themselves to school.

Once the children have made the transition into a new school day, they participate in a more formal "circle time." Marshall reads books, they sing songs, and perform a number of ritualized learning activities as they note the date on the calendar.

In Fresno, California, Deborah Manning writes about how her first grade students take responsibility for opening ceremonies (Manning and Fennacy 1993). After the children have hung up their coats, signed in, checked the message board, and chosen the books from the classroom library that they will read later, they gather on the rug and await directions from the child in charge. Manning describes the ritual of a typical ceremony.

> Patricia, the child in charge, checks her clipboard for the names of the two children she recorded the previous day. She calls on them one at a time. First Nicki shares his intricate Lego construction, then Chelsea shows everyone her tooth that fell out the night before. Each sharing leads to numerous comments and questions from the audience. Patricia then invites volunteers for tomorrow's sharing and writes down their names. Next, she checks her clipboard to see who might want to read an entry from their classroom journals. Two children read the entries they wrote the night before. After responding to comments and questions from their classmates, they select volunteers who will take the journals home next.

The ritual continues. Another child who is in charge of class business takes the lead next. The child selects and signs up volunteers for the two class typewriters, the reading loft, and the listening center; and also fills in the attendance form, takes lunch count, and heads for the office to turn them in. All this time, Manning has been part of the class audience—listening and responding—but not interfering. Once the child-leaders have completed their responsibilities, Manning moves to the front of the circle and engages the children in a round of songs and shared reading. Then she sends them off to read the books they selected earlier. The day has begun.

*Field Notes: Teacher-To-Teacher*

Each day we start over and give each other a chance to change, grow, and learn. Problems from yesterday disappear when you walk in the door. You can be whoever you want to be today. Assumptions are always positive.

*Chris Boyd*
*Roadrunner School*
*Phoenix, Arizona*

Martha Ahlman teaches a multigrade-multiage group of Navajo children, ranging in age from 5 1/2 to 9, first to fourth grade. She and her students share a morning ceremony that begins with talk about upcoming events, personal and public news, and the weather. They sing songs, make patterns (long-hair, short-hair braids), and create a group graph. After their Navajo lesson from Ahlman's aide, it's story time—Ahlman reads a storybook or a chapter from a chapter book. The ceremony ends with discussion about the expectations for the day. "This time gets everyone into gear for the day," explains Ahlman, "and the children know what to expect."

**Celebrations and ending the day.** Many other rituals and ceremonies make up the fabric of a school day. Janice Marshall and her students in Tucson celebrate birthdays with a special birthday ceremony. They light candles, sing several birthday songs, and read birthday books. Wearing a glittery birthday crown that he or she has made and designed, the birthday child calls on classmates who ask a range of personal questions related to the child's life and birthday. Lost teeth call for another ceremony. When a child arrives with a new window in their smiles, they write their name on the tooth graph and add a paper tooth with their name on it to a special tooth necklace for the tooth fairy.

*Rituals and ceremonies, whether spontaneous or planned, help bind the class together as a community.*

Chris Boyd's kindergartners follow a ritual for ending their day. Everyone becomes very quiet and thinks about the learning day they've shared together. What worked well for them? What didn't work as well? What can they do to have a better day tomorrow? On paper, they sketch their ideas. Later, if they want, they can share their pictures with a partner. This time out for quiet reflection at day's end has become a ritual that the kinders look forward to. In fact, Boyd says, if it's cancelled, they complain. It helps to tie loose ends together, and brings the class together to end on a harmonious note. It also helps set the tone for the next day as children consider ways to improve their classroom life.

Rituals and ceremonies, whether spontaneous or planned, help bind the class together as a community. Within the context of ceremony, even ordinary acts such as taking attendance or noting the date on the calendar take on symbolic meaning. All members can anticipate and participate in the comfortable, familiar sequence of events. These shared, symbolic experiences create an internal order, harmonizing classroom life.

---

### DIALOGUE

How do I begin and end my school day? _____

_____

What ceremonies do I have? _____

_____

How can I use more effectively the community-building tools of ceremony and ritual?

_____

---

### SHOPTALK

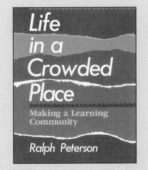

Peterson, Ralph. *Life in a Crowded Place: Making a Learning Community*. Portsmouth, New Hampshire: Heinemann, 1992.

No one will deny that life in classrooms is an intense social experience. Crowded together with students for six or more hours a day in a space no bigger than a large living room, the natural response of most people would be to maintain control and enforce obedience. But creating a community—bringing students together and keeping them together—is the most vital aspect of a teacher's work. Without it, real learning cannot take place, as even the most sound philosophies and techniques amount to little without a community to bring them to life. The concept of community in the classroom is certainly not new, but little has been written about what makes up a community, how it is created, and what functions it fulfills. Peterson aims—and succeeds—in showing how to make a community that influences the quality of learning and life in elementary and middle schools.

### The Art of Discipline

*Webster's* offers two general meanings of discipline. One has to do with "submission to authority"; the other with "training that develops self-control, character, or orderliness and efficiency." In a learner-centered classroom, the emphasis is on the latter definition. We strive to help our students create an internal focus of control, to take the initiative, think for themselves, and assume responsibility for their own learning and behavior. Again, there are specific strategies we can use to achieve this.

But first a word about boredom. Before we blame our students for being an out-of-control bunch of hooligans, we need to take a hard look at our curriculum. Simple boredom is often the root cause of discipline problems. As Susan Ohanian (1982) states, "There's only one true technique for good discipline and that's good curriculum." When kids are involved with a project that engages their interest and learning passion, they are much less likely to act up and act out. "When a kid is in trouble in my class," writes Susan, "I don't change the way I smile—I alter the child's curriculum."

*In a learner-centered classroom, students create an internal focus of control, take the initiative, think for themselves, and assume responsibility for their own learning and behavior.*

Assuming your curriculum is rich, offering children meaningful learning experiences, let's take a look at strategies that help children learn the self-responsibility that creates a peaceful, productive classroom learning community.

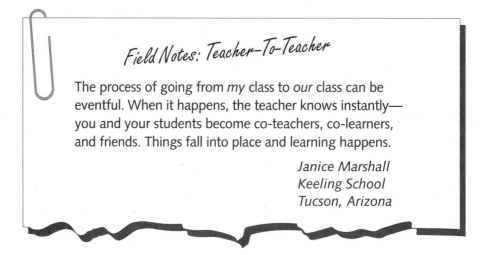

*Field Notes: Teacher-To-Teacher*

The process of going from *my* class to *our* class can be eventful. When it happens, the teacher knows instantly—you and your students become co-teachers, co-learners, and friends. Things fall into place and learning happens.

*Janice Marshall*
*Keeling School*
*Tucson, Arizona*

**Norms for living and learning.** The big ideas that govern life and learning in Nan Mohr's upper elementary classroom are courtesy, safety, and responsibility. She weaves them throughout her curriculum, breathing conceptual life into them. "How did a particular scientist, inventor, or writer solve a problem or conflict? What happened when Spain and England wanted gold and spices in the New World, or when both royal houses wanted to be first?"

Mohr helps her students arrive at these norms through a series of brainstorming sessions. "We brainstorm ideas and words about norms and ways we are and act in Room 10. We make lists of actions and describing words which are up on chart paper for several days. Students are free to add pictures or words which describe 'the way we want to be' and 'how we want to act.' A marker is kept near the charts and students may add to them as they think of other descriptions of our 'dream for Room 10.' These lists come in handy all year. We use them to review and evaluate our progress as a learning community. Norms may be adjusted and changed as needed."

*Field Notes: Teacher-To-Teacher*

Fostering self-responsiblity is the central element of my curriculum. It crosses over into every social and academic area. I stress over and over, overtly and loudly, that the only person responsible for your learning and your behavior is *you*! When an issue arises that requires clear, individual student buy-in, I will ask each student individually if he or she understands the responsibility. This eye-to-eye personalization of the action is powerful. It is time-consuming and intense, but well worth the effort.

*Greg Chapnick*
*Charquin School*
*Hayward, California*

Greg Chapnick teaches in a multigrade classroom, kindergarten through sixth grade, at Charquin, an alternative public school in Hayward, California. Like Mohr, Chapnick keeps his norms for behavior simple and positive:

- Respect everyone.
- Listen carefully.
- Try your hardest.
- Ask questions.

He finds that class meetings are an invaluable forum for solving group problems. Chapnick explains how the problem-solving meetings work: "I facilitate the meetings. The structure is relatively loose. The item on the agenda is explained; comments are made about the situation; solutions are brainstormed and voted upon if appropriate. Subjects include large group problems, use of athletic equipment, planning class projects, or field trips. Class meetings are usually a time-consuming process, and do not always solve the issue directly. The process is an empowering, democratic model for the children. I never consider it a waste of time, even when the issue at hand does not get resolved cleanly."

Field Notes: Teacher-To-Teacher

We live by three simple rules in our kindergarten classroom.

1. Use inside voices (to prevent headaches).

2. Use walking feet (to prevent headaches and other aches).

3. Take care of people and things (our most important rule).

Our goal is to have a safe place to learn. As the year goes by and the children are more aware and responsible, the room is governed by one question: Do we have a safe place to learn? "Make it so!" straight from Captain Picard of the *Starship Enterprise*.

*Chris Boyd*
*Roadrunner School*
*Phoenix, Arizona*

Mary Kitagawa finds five, positively-stated rules work best for her and her fifth graders:

- Respond to directions immediately; if no directions are given, use your head.
- Speak respectfully.
- Show physical self-control.
- Help keep materials in order.
- Allow others to learn and teach.

Kitagawa offers additional advice. Keep things playful. Have fun. She uses a toy frog to croak at the kids when she needs their attention. Her colleague next door uses a kazoo. Both have the same effect. "The silliness of it all gets the kids laughing—and listening!" For similar results, try singing. Don Howard, a veteran teacher in an inner city Chicago school, has song banners hanging from the ceiling of his classroom on which he's printed the lyrics of favorite songs and raps. Whenever he needs the kids' attention—or to signal a transition into a new activity—he simply chooses a song from one of the banners and bursts into song. The kids join in. Soon everyone is involved and tuned-in.

Of course, there are days when, in spite of all our careful, sensitive planning, things go awry. We have bad days. Kids do, too. When that happens, kids may need a time out. For this purpose, Kitagawa keeps a desk at the back of the room equipped with several "toys." "One toy is a fascinating timer that spirals green bubbles down chutes, taking about three minutes to reach the bottom. It's very calming. If I say 'take a time out' to someone, or if someone feels angry and wants a time out, the desk and timer are available. Anyone can play with the timer or sit at the desk at any time. The advantage is that three minutes isn't too long, and I don't have to monitor the time. Any time after the timer finishes, the time out is over. I also keep *Where's Waldo* books and *Where's Waldo* toys and a set of books about snakes that can hold anyone's interest." As Kitagawa explains, the toys and books are for anyone at any time, but they also serve to make the time out less punitive and more relaxing. A calm, relaxed student is more likely to experience a changed attitude.

## SHOPTALK

Nelsen, Jane. *Positive Discipline*. New York: Ballantine Books, 1987.

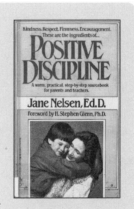

Nelson discusses "natural consequences"—what happens naturally under certain circumstances versus "logical consequences"— what we do to teach, not punish, when natural consequences are unsafe or undesirable. This goes from running in a crowd (it's unsafe to let you get hurt) to not doing work (it's undesirable to let you not learn). At all times there is an effort to make sure that logical consequences are related, reasonable, and respectful. Otherwise it's punishment. Discipline is teaching. Punishment is painful. The idea is to be firm but kind.

### We Can Solve It!
Problem solving is a key ingredient in effective learner-centered classrooms. "Discipline consists of problem solving to make the classroom a safe place to learn," states Chris Boyd, "not to follow a checksheet of rules. When there is a problem, we change the situation; we don't punish the child. Therefore, children behave because that works best, not because they are afraid they might get their names on the board."

Many successful teachers use conflict resolution strategies to help their students learn how to negotiate, compromise, and reach solutions that all can live with. Barbara Porro, an expert in the field who conducts workshops on conflict resolution, offers the following guidelines.

### Tips on Helping Children Resolve Their Conflicts

1. Listen for fact and feelings.

   • Ask child #1: *What's the problem? How are you feeling?*

   Restate: *So you're _____ because _____.*
                  (feeling)            (specific behavior)

   • Ask child #2: *What's the problem? How are you feeling?*

   Restate: *So you're _____ because _____.*
                  (feeling)            (specific behavior)

   • If necessary, ask questions to clarify what children are saying.

   • Define the problem. Summarize in terms of need.

   *So it sounds like #1 needs _____ and #2 needs _____, right?*

2. Help children brainstorm possible solutions.

   • Ask both: *What could you do to solve the problem?*

   • Elicit ideas as quickly as possible without comments. Keep track of children's ideas. If there are lots of ideas, write them down.

   • Accept all ideas without making judgments.

   • Keep children's attention focused on developing solutions.

   *Yes, you could _____. What else could you try?*

3. Help children choose and plan.

   • Ask: *Which idea works best for both of you?*

   • Help children choose a win-win solution.

   • Ask questions that elicit a specific action plan.

   *What will you do next? What needs to happen first? then what?*

   *How are you going to _____? when? where? who?*

4. Help children reflect and evaluate.

   • Later, ask: *How did your solution work?*

   • If successful, offer congratulations. If not, plan for more problem solving.

**Writing for solutions.** Peggy Smullin, a second-grade teacher at Fair Oaks School in Redwood City, California, recommends that children write their way into a solution. She has developed a problem-solving form. The procedure for using the form is simple.

- Explain to children that when they have a problem of any sort, self-created or stemming from a disagreement with another child, they are to take a problem-solving form (stored in a box in a convenient classroom location) and fill it out. They may use invented spelling, drawings, or labels to complete it.
- Once the form is completed, they slip it into the problem-solving binder (kept near the forms).
- At least once a week, during the class meeting, you and the children can review the problem-solving forms and discuss the different solutions that the children have come up with.

The end result? Rather than coming to you for help with every little dilemma (and there are many during the course of a normal school day), children assume responsibility for finding solutions to their own problems. When they do bump heads with another child, they know it's time to take and complete a form. They may choose to complete it together or each submit their own. Writing is therapy. Once children have broken free of a troublesome situation, and can spend a quiet moment reflecting on what happened, why it happened, and how they might solve it, they are often able to write through to a solution.

When the forms are shared during a class meeting, children are exposed to a variety of problem-solving strategies—some more effective than others—but the opportunity to talk and negotiate is important. What are the effective ways to solve our problems? What can we learn from each other? How can we all help each other work through our problems?

---

**Problem-Solving Form**

Name_____ Date_____

I have a problem _____

_____

_____

Possible solutions _____

_____

_____

**Talking out a solution.** Talking out a solution is another effective problem-solving strategy. Bonnie Laster teaches kindergarten at Castro School in Mountain View, California. Almost every one of her students is a non-native speaker of English. Bonnie recommends these steps:

- Find a small rug. (I use a Winnie-the-Pooh rug.) Keep it rolled up in a convenient spot in the classroom.
- When two kids have a disagreement about something, they know to get the rug, put it down in an out-of-the-way spot in the classroom, and then sit on it facing each other.
- After they have vented their anger, they should begin to explain to each other how they are feeling, why they got angry, and together, work at finding a solution.
- There are only two rules: 1) No hitting; and 2) You have to keep talking until you find a solution you both feel good about.

Children will quickly understand how to use the rug if you demonstrate for them with another adult or child how to talk through to a solution. After two or three demonstrations, children will be ready for the learning powers of the rug! Remind them that it is their responsibility to get the rug when they need it; they don't have to ask you first.

**Puppets and role-playing.** Janice Marshall reports that her students work through conflicts with dinosaur puppets she keeps on hand for that purpose. They use the STOP technique.

- Stop
- Think about behavior
- Options, what are they?
- Plan what to do.

Marshall admits that it takes a lot of time and effort—and a lot of spur-of-the-moment learning and teaching—but it pays off. In this way, everything is viewed as a learning experience.

## S H O P T A L K

Gibbs, Jeanne. *Tribes*. Santa Rosa, California: Center Source Publications, 1987.

Are you a teacher who feels the need for more structure in your classroom, but can't abide the mindless control of assertive discipline? *Tribes* offers a management process that new teachers in particular may find reassuring. The handbook provides detailed instructions and theory to help teachers create positive learning environments and collaborative learning groups. It promises that kids will learn genuine mutual regard, interaction skills, and responsibility.

## Celebrations

Plenty of good things happen in classrooms. Joshua and Jeremy work together to find the solution to a math puzzle; Tami shares her lunch with Ben who forgot his; René feels comfortable enough to share during the family meeting—a first! It's important to recognize and celebrate these happy events. Second-grade teacher Peggy Smullin recognizes happy events in her classroom with "Celebrations" forms. These forms work in much the same way as the problem-solving forms do. Kids may take and complete one whenever they recognize a celebration. The form also asks them to think about how they'd like to share the celebration with their classmates. They may choose to draw a picture, write a story, poem, or song, or perform a puppet show, skit, or dance. The completed forms can be stored in a celebrations binder.

Celebrations

Name _____ Date _____

Something good happened _____

_____

How I'd like to share the celebration _____

_____

_____

## S H O P T A L K

Goodman, Kenneth S., Lois Bridges Bird and Yetta M. Goodman, eds. *The Whole Language Catalog.* New York: SRA: Macmillan/McGraw-Hill, 1991.

*The Whole Language Catalog* is a one-volume resource library of 448 oversized pages packed with

- nuts and bolts ideas from experienced learner-centered educators
- hundreds of curriculum and professional resources
- explanations of language and learner-centered education by internationally respected authorities
- lively, informative history of progressive education
- candid photographs, funny anecdotes, and inspiring first-person stories of and by teachers, parents, students, administrators, researchers, and others—that will make you laugh and think.

*The Whole Language Catalog* will inform, guide, entertain, and inspire. It's a celebration of caring, hardworking teachers and parents who have dedicated their lives to bringing all students humane and democratic education.

*Chapter 3*
# Have a Look Around

I'm a passionate bookstore browser. When a rare free moment arises, there's nothing I like better than spending an hour or two in my favorite bookstore. Although I love to read, it's not just the books that draw me. It's the whole atmosphere. My bookstore is housed in a bright, lofty room. Striking art adorns the walls: Picasso, Chagall, and Van Gogh prints; vibrant African weavings; and Tohono O'odham "maze of life" baskets. Graceful ferns hang from the ceiling, and soft classical music adds to a feeling of peace and comfort. And everywhere there are signs, posters, book displays, magazines, newspapers, photographs—all sorts of interesting things to read.

The same elements that make my favorite bookstore such an inviting place belong in a classroom as well. Just because classrooms are inside institutional public buildings doesn't mean that they have to look and feel like an institution. Think about the purpose of classrooms. They are supposed to be places to learn, and think, and explore, and discover. How much creative learning and thinking could you do sitting for seven hours at a small, hard desk surrounded by walls plastered with colored construction paper? As you plan the physical set-up of your classroom, consider aesthetic appeal, space and organization that enables comfortable, free-flowing movement, and a design that evokes warmth and security.

### Getting Physical

Consider the furniture arrangement. In learner-centered classrooms, students are encouraged to work together. It hardly makes sense, then, to keep them in separate desks, separate from each other in rows. Work tables are best. But if you are stuck with desks, you can push them together. Some teachers prefer a horseshoe shape. In that way, everyone can see and talk with everyone else. But whatever arrangement you choose, classroom furniture should facilitate student interaction and collaboration, not impede it.

Greg Chapnick, a multigrade teacher in Hayward, California, works at Charquin, an alternative public school that gave up desks twenty years ago in favor of work tables. The tables are arranged to facilitate movement, collaborative groupings, and Chapnick's ability to reach everyone. "Tables work much better than desks," Chapnick reports. "I'd never go back to desks unless I had to."

Mary Kitagawa, a multigrade teacher in Amherst, Massachusetts, uses clipboards to facilitate writing without a desk. Students are free to find the best space in which to work. The desks serve mainly as places to keep things. Kitagawa admits that even her desk is just a repository. "I have no chair at it, and it's always too cluttered to work on. It does, however, give me a place to stack things—or to say to a student, 'Put it on my desk.'"

*Field Notes: Teacher-To-Teacher*

We meet near the library because I like the feel of being surrounded by books. Also, I need easy access to the books so I can grab one as things come up in our discussions that call for clarification. Then children can see where I put the book back in case they want to read it themselves later.

*Chris Boyd*
*Roadrunner School*
*Phoenix, Arizona*

### Teacher Space

There's a joke about teachers in learner-centered classrooms: when you step inside their classrooms, you can't find them. That's because they're not sitting behind a big desk apart from their students; they are on the floor, conferencing with a small group about their portfolios, hidden behind a puppet theater helping a group with the final touches before the big show, or sitting at a work table conducting an individual reading conference.

*Field Notes: Teacher-To-Teacher*

No one has ownership of any particular seat or place in our classroom. We are constantly working in different groups and we just put tables together or separate them according to need.

*Martha Ahlmann*
*Chuska School*
*Tohatchi, New Mexico*

Even though you may not spend much time at your desk, you still need space to call your own. Greg Chapnick tries to establish a special, personal space for himself. "I put up pictures of famous people who have influenced me or whom I admire, and a few personal things just to make me feel at home." Chris Boyd establishes a teacher-resource area where she keeps her records and supplies: files, class sets of books, a typewriter, and a variety of curriculum supplies. This area "provides easy access for me as I prepare for class or if I need to pull out something for a spontaneous learning situation," Boyd explains. "Time is very limited and 'hunting time' is not a luxury I can afford."

DIALOGUE

As you consider how to make your classroom an inviting and comfortable place, consider your own needs.

What do I find comforting? stimulating? In what sort of environment do I learn best?

_____

_____

What do my students like?

_____

_____

How can I bring these elements into my classroom?

_____

_____

Try your hand at a new classroom design. You may want to visit your colleagues' classrooms; together, pool your ideas to create a learner-centered look and feel.

## Learning Centers

Next, think about work areas. As a student teacher in the 70s, I learned to love learning centers. In addition to my classroom library, I always had a science center, math and discovery center, a drama and dress-up center, and a listening center. I found that the centers allowed children to interact, share, and cooperate with each other. They worked and learned together. And collecting materials was easier, too. All I needed were supplies to stock each center which accommodated about six children at a time. Six scales for the math center met our needs, rather than 30 scales, one for each child.

Let's take a closer look at these individual areas or centers. How do they work? What do you need? How do you get started?

First, you can use centers in a variety of ways. You'll want to experiment and see what works best for you. You may want to use the centers as extra learning experiences. Once children have finished their core curriculum activities, they can spend time working at a center of their choice. Or you may make centers an integral part of your overall program. Once your students are working in centers, you circulate, observe them at work, and step in to offer help as needed.

---

### D I A L O G U E

As you think about how you might use learning centers in your classroom, here are some questions to consider.

How will I use centers—as places for extra activities? as the central organizer for my curriculum?

_____

_____

What sorts of centers would work best for me? What should each center contain? What should I name them?

_____

_____

How many do I need? _____

_____

Where will I set up the centers? _____

_____

How many children can participate at a center at one time?

_____

What materials do I need? How will I store supplies? Where will children keep their center projects?

_____

_____

---

*Learning centers allow children to interact, share, and cooperate with each other.*

Here are suggestions for different kinds of centers and the sorts of materials each might require. Adapt and change them to fit your students' and your own needs and interests. I recommend

- taking time to thoroughly introduce each center, explaining the learning tasks, materials, and expected outcomes
- introducing each center at different times so kids don't overload on explanatory information
- allowing time for sharing after each learning center time. Invite kids to come together and talk about their experiences with each center. Together, as a group, you can evaluate each center. What is working well? What isn't working as well? How can you revise the centers to make them more effective?
- working out a rotation system or tracking sheet for students so that both you and they can keep track of their center work.

*Every class needs a central meeting area where everyone can gather comfortably.*

A note about materials: for each center, I've included a wish list. In the ideal world, these materials would be yours. But the ideal and reality are different; indeed, some teachers feel fortunate when they have paper for their students. Don't despair. A little money and a lot of ingenuity will serve you in good stead. Let parents know what you need. They may be willing to donate materials or help you raise money through bake sales or car washes to purchase needed supplies. My enterprising teacher friends have asked local businesses to adopt their classroom. Everyone wins. Businesses feel good about supporting local teachers and children. Teachers and kids certainly feel good about getting equipment and materials they need.

**Whole Group Meeting Area**
Every class needs a central meeting area where everyone can gather comfortably. Visualize yourself visiting with your friends. Where are you sitting? Probably not on a cold, tile floor! Your students won't want to sit there either. So as you plan this area, think about what you can do to make it warm, cozy, and comfortable. Many carpet stores will donate large remnants to classroom teachers. Check garage sales or thrift stores for large area rugs. Other possibilities for your meeting area include old sofas, beanbag chairs, large pillows, and rocking chairs. This area needs to be big enough to seat all the children in a circle so they can see each other during discussions.

**Art Studio**
Art is messy. It works best near water. Set up your art studio near the classroom sink. If your floors are covered with carpet, put a shower curtain, painting tarp, or something washable to catch paint spills and glue drips. In *Visual*

*Arts as a Way of Knowing* (forthcoming), Karolynne Gee offers detailed information for creating a classroom art center.

There are many wonderful children's books available now about art, including biographies of famous painters, how-to-draw books, and techniques for different media. As you begin to build a classroom art library, consider storing such books in your art studio for quick reference and inspiration.

You'll want to display children's artistic creations. If you are low on open wall space, try clothespins and clothesline stretched from wall to wall for an instant aerial gallery. Kindergarten teacher Chris Boyd makes room in her art gallery for an individual student's art show. Budding artists in the room sign up for their own show. They display art they've completed at school as well as their artistic creations from home. Every artist is given time to explain his or her show to the class.

**What to wish for**
- crayons, felt-tip markers, chalk, charcoal, pencils, pens
- watercolors, oil pastels, and brushes
- paper of all sorts, colors, sizes
- glue, paste, masking tape, glue sticks
- cotton tips
- fabric scraps, magazines that can be cut up, yarn

*Field Notes: Teacher-To-Teacher*

I provide children with a wide range of media to express ideas. We learn many art techniques and incorporate them into our bookmaking.

*Janice Marshall*
*Keeling School*
*Tucson, Arizona*

**Math Exploration**

I was great at math until geometry. That's when my one math learning strategy—memorization—failed me. You can't memorize geometry. You have to understand it. Susan Ohanian, author of *Math as a Way of Knowing* (1995), shows you how to make math not only understandable, but intriguing, challenging, and fun. Educators Heidi Mills, David Whitin, and Timothy O'Keefe (1991) offer five guidelines for creating authentic mathematical experiences. Follow them and your students are more likely to really understand mathematical language, concepts, and computation.

1. Make the problems open-ended; invite children to solve problems in a variety of ways and to interpret them from a variety of perspectives.

2. Invite kids to adapt and change the problems. They can do so, often with ingenious results.

3. Encourage children to explore using a variety of communication systems: art, music, writing, drama, reading, and mathematics. Numbers do not operate in a vacuum. They gain meaning as they work in conjunction with other communication systems.

4. Take risks! Children grow in mathematical literacy when they take risks and step outside the sphere of what they know by testing out a new hunch or a current hypothesis about how numbers work.

5. Encourage collaboration. Children learn from each other as they share observations and insights about how to construct and share meaning in mathematics.

**What to wish for**

- manipulatives of all sorts: pattern blocks, attribute blocks, tangrams, Cuisenaire rods, Unifix cubes, dice, geoboards
- junk materials for sorting, counting, and classifying
- recording sheets

- graph paper
- measuring tools: scales, balances, rulers
- geometric shapes
- literature books with math themes
- calculators, old adding machines

## S H O P T A L K

Whitin, David, Heidi Mills and Timothy O'Keefe. *Living and Learning Mathematics: Stories and Strategies for Supporting Mathematical Literacy*. Portsmouth, New Hampshire: Heinemann, 1991.

Here's a book that supports what veteran learner-centered teachers have always known: learning mathematics is a process much like learning to read and write. The book identifies strategies that children use as they construct their own mathematical stories and investigations, lists characteristics of learning experiences that promote mathematical literacy, and provides a framework for making curriculum decisions. The author's whole language recommendations, well documented through numerous photographs and examples of children's work, emphasize interdisciplinary themes of study and children's interests as a framework for curriculum development.

## Science and Technology Center

I confess that as a new teacher, my science program didn't extend much beyond charting the growth of lima beans or showing occasional afternoon filmstrips with titles like "Our Friends, the Earthworms." To me, science seemed scary. But I finally did discover that I could enjoy it. Folks at the National Science Resource Center, who certainly know and love science, say this:

> We...believe that children begin to learn science from the moment they start to perceive their environment, that they have an innate need to make sense of what happens. They make assumptions based on their perceptions, and they begin to predict what will happen and to test their predictions. Bit by bit, they form a useful model of the world around them. Before children go to school, they exercise their natural curiosity daily. School can expand their universe and open new areas of inquiry for them. Or it can close off their search for knowledge by presenting science as a set of words and rules to be memorized from the pages of a textbook (National Academy Press 1990).

## SHOPTALK

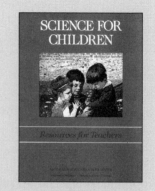

National Academy Press. *Science for Children: Resources for Teachers.* Washington, DC: National Academy Press, 1990.

Across the country, there seems to be a renewed interest in elementary science education. With the interest comes many questions of when, where, and how to extend elementary science beyond the traditional textbook-centered approach. Fortunately, help is near, and the perfect place to begin is with *Science for Children*. This guide describes curriculum materials and sources of information that can provide excellent support for effective, hands-on, inquiry-based programs. The guide is divided into three major sections: curriculum materials (offers an annotated bibliography of most of the major science curriculum projects), supplementary resources (includes annotated listings of science activity books, methods books, and magazines for children and teachers), and sources of information and assistance (offers institutional resources such as museums, technology centers, professional organizations, publishers, and suppliers).

Mike McGuffee, a Christa McAuliffe Fellow and elementary teacher in Stillwater, Oklahoma, agrees. He works with school districts across the country developing hands-on science programs. McGuffee recommends keeping the science focus simple and taking instructional cues from the students. One of his own science experiences illustrates his point.

> My fourth grade class completed a unit of activities called Clay Boats. They were given a ball of clay and a beaker of water and were asked to drop the clay into the water and record their observations. The clay sank to the bottom and a discussion followed. Next, students were asked to try to make the clay float. They eventually realized that a boat or saucer shape would float, and the class took off. They tried to get their boats to carry cargo: pennies, paper clips, and washers. They made many comparisons between the shapes of the boats and their cargo-carrying capacities.

After they had completed a dozen activities, McGuffee asked another question that led to more experimentation and discovery: What happened to make the clay float when you reshaped it?

As McGuffee says in his article "Hands-On Science" (1991), "Teaching in this manner wakes us from the sleepy world of traditional science. It adds a dimension of playfulness to school that follows the natural course of childhood. Leaving behind the familiar, it allows us to risk, not always knowing our destination. Taking this journey can inspire excitement and a renewed sense of wonder about our universe."

**What to wish for**

- magnifying glasses
- wonders that children have found
- recording sheets for observations
- things that float and sink
- toolbox
- empty plastic bottles
- cardboard
- locks and keys
- pulleys, levers
- old machines for students to
  take apart (bicycle, eggbeater, etc.)
- tape
- wire
- batteries
- magnets
- string
- flashlight bulbs
- plastic tubing
- wood scraps
- straws
- water
- balloons

**Drama and Puppet Theater**

Paul Heller, a drama teacher in Benicia, California, and the author of *Drama as a Way of Knowing* (1995), recognizes that the thought of classroom drama can make teachers nervous, but he offers this comforting advice:

> Drama, I know, sounds like hard work. And it is if you do for the students what they can do for themselves. If you write the scripts, make the costumes and scenery, worry about making it snow indoors, you could be up all night for weeks. But the great thing about drama is that students can create and manipulate every aspect of it. Realizing this is the first step to making drama easy and fun.

Drama can begin by simply creating an area in the classroom for it to happen. Canadian teachers, Jane Baskwill and Paulette Whitman, who team teach a primary, multigrade class in Nova Scotia, place their drama center near the library so that children can find the stories they are enacting and refer to the original text for guidance. Chris Boyd combines three centers: drama, housekeeping, and large blocks in her kindergarten. In this way, building blocks can be incorporated into the dramatic play. The housekeeping theme changes monthly. Matching props and costumes encourages new play. One month it's a hospital; another, a store (well-stocked with empty food containers and decorated with store signs). Other possibilities include a firehouse, post office, or castle. There's no limit. Let your students use their imaginations.

**What to wish for**

- puppet theater, easily made from refrigerator box
- variety of puppets, handmade as well as commercial
- puppet-making materials you may want to house in the art studio: cardboard, sticks, paper bags, old socks, buttons, bits of fabric
- props of all sorts, such as a toy castle, house, airport, garage
- telephones
- masks, commercial and handmade
- dress-up clothes (check thrift stores and garage sales)

*Field Notes: Teacher-To-Teacher*

There is a time and place for scripts, but drama without scripts is fun and more freeing. If the children know the story, the characters, and the sequence of action, whether they say the exact words each time will not matter as they act out a tale. Every child will know what is needed and what must be done to move the story along. The children's ideas are valued and accepted, so they develop a real sense of ownership of the story.

*Sheryl McGruder*
*Fairview Elementary School*
*Columbia, Missouri*

*We have a responsibility as educators to acquaint ourselves with children's and adolescent's literature and to build classroom libraries.*

**Classroom Library**

When was the last time a basal reader made you weep? But who among us has not shed a tear over Katherine Paterson's *Bridge to Terabithia*, laughed over Judith Viorst's *Alexander and the Terrible, Horrible, No Good, Very Bad Day*, or smiled with gratitude for our friends, after reading, once again, E.B. White's *Charlotte's Web*. There are more than 3,000 new children's literature titles published every year. It makes no sense to introduce children to the joys of reading with poorly written or condensed material.

**Literature connections.** We have a responsibility as professional educators to acquaint ourselves with children's and adolescent's literature. I would go one step further and say we have a professional responsibility to build classroom libraries. But, as one who has lived lean years on a teacher's salary, I would never say we have to use our own money to purchase books (although I did and many, many teachers do). Don't let a shortage of funds prevent you from living a rich, full life in the world of literature. There are ways to build a terrific library (your most valuable teaching tool), and not go broke doing it.

Vera Milz, a veteran primary teacher of more than thirty years in Bloomfield Hills, Michigan, is one of the most remarkable teachers I know. She has an international reputation as a teacher who knows kids, knows literature, and puts the two together in magical ways. Here's her guide to creating a big classroom library with a small resource budget.

### Vera Milz's Guide to Getting Children's Books at the Lowest Possible Cost

If your community has a strong school and public library system, perhaps you can borrow enough books to keep your children reading. However, I like to have these books available in my classroom for children to check out and begin to form the habit of locating. I also want to be able to introduce a book, and have it in the classroom library so that children can read it at their leisure. In 30 years of collecting books, and over 5,000 books later, these are some of my sources.

**Book clubs.** This has been my mainstay. I save dividend points, and have used them to purchase books in single copies, or sets. Most of my big books have also come from this resource. Read the monthly flyer for one-time offers. Also, end-of-the-year clearances are real bargains.

**Teacher kits.** If your district is locked into a basal program, there still may be some money available for supplemental materials. Kits, such as *Scholastic's Bookshelf,* may be something you can convince a district to purchase. The main problem is that you get a preselected set of books—yet, if you are careful in choosing the set you want, most of the books should fit your needs.

**Birthday books and teacher gifts.** Instead of a food item, I suggest that children consider giving a book to the classroom for a birthday treat. If a book is given, we read the book together, and it is added to our library with a bookplate remembering the child's birthday and year in our room. If you teach in an area where teachers are given holiday gifts, you might consider asking your room parent to pass the word that you would appreciate a book for the classroom rather than a personal gift.

**Share-a-book.** A beginning teacher and one of my colleagues, Mary Anne Callaghan, wanted a classroom library quickly, so she asked parents to buy a book for the children to share for the year. She keeps available a list of "wish books" with the discounted prices from a local distributor, for parents to choose from. During the school year, the books are circulated each evening, and children check out "their book," as well as many others. At the end of the year, children can take the book their family purchased home or contribute it to the classroom library. If the book is left, when it is read the next year, the class sends a thank you note to the child who donated it. In a few years of teaching, Callaghan has a library of several hundred books. In addition, she often receives book gift certificates from parents who are excited about their child's developing love of reading.

**Garage sales.** I check out the neighborhood garage sales over the summer, and have found quite a few good books that children have outgrown but are perfect for my classroom.

**Used book stores.** I buy most of my own paperback books from these stores, and I always check the children's sections. They don't have a lot, but I have found some useful books over the years.

**Library sales.** My neighborhood library holds book sales on Saturday mornings during the winter. These are books that are starting to wear out with heavy usage, or donated books that the library already has. They are all sold at bargain prices, and are great for classroom use.

**Remaindered books.** I always check the table of bargain books at the big chains or the independent bookstores. To avoid tax penalties on warehoused books, often great books are dumped on the market at very low prices. You never know what treasures you may find.

**Book stores.** I know the discount every store in my area has for teachers. In addition, there are several distribution centers that allow me to purchase books on my own at thirty five and forty percent discounts if I can get a school purchase order. Ask questions. It's amazing how much you can save.

**Book supplies.** To make books, I ask parents to donate a roll of contact paper for classroom use. I also ask them to save pieces of cardboard from the front and back of cereal boxes, and to watch for sources of cardboard for bookmaking purposes.

**Conferences and conventions.** If you attend the National Council of Teachers of English, or International Reading Association annual conventions, join the chaos of the closing book sales. Many of the trade book publishers sell their samples for half price. It's crazy to go from booth to booth, but I have purchased some wonderful books in this way.

**Choosing and using children's books: informational resources**
Christopher-Gordon Publishers, Inc.
480 Washington Street
Norwood, Massachusetts 02062
Journals: *The New Advocate, Perspectives*

The Horn Book, Inc.
14 Beacon Street
Boston, Massachusetts 02108-9765
Journals: *The Horn Book, The Horn Book Guide*

International Reading Association
800 Barksdale Road, PO Box 8139
Newark, Delaware 19714-8139
Journal: *The Reading Teacher*

National Council of Teachers of English
1111 Kenyon Road
Urbana, Illinois 61801
Journal: *Language Arts*

Richard C. Owen Publishers, Inc.
135 Katonah Avenue
Katonah, New York 10536
Newsletter: *Teacher's Networking*

*Field Notes: Teacher-To-Teacher*

I have a large library of individual titles (about 500) and literature study sets (70 or so titles). I got most of them through book clubs or at used book stores. I think it's important to offer lots of choices for reading material. We've organized our books alphabetically—at kid height.

*Greg Chapnick*
*Charquin School*
*Hayward, California*

Why not dream big when designing and creating your classroom library? It's been said that if a teacher did nothing but spend the day reading to her students she would succeed and succeed nobly. Your classroom library is your greatest teaching resource, deserving of your most potent professional dreams. Here's an additional wish list to help make your dreams come true.

**What to wish for**

- reading lofts; every classroom in my own children's school, Ohlone Elementary in Palo Alto, California, has a parent-constructed reading loft. Every loft is well-stocked with books, pillows, posters—like my favorite bookstore six feet up—great places to get lost in a book.
- claw-foot bathtubs; if you can find them, they make for cozy reading. Fill them with pillows and comforters.

- sets of books for literature study; about six copies of each title work best.
- individual titles of both fiction and nonfiction.
- subscriptions to a wide variety of children's literary, science, and project magazines such as *Stone Soup, Ranger Rick*, and *Highlights*.
- an organizational system for using and maintaining the library.

Mary Kitagawa offers these guidelines for a smooth-running classroom library:

> My classroom library comprises seven or eight hundred books, mostly paperbacks. I have put little pockets inside the front covers and have index cards in the pockets. Each card has the author's initial in a circle, if it's fiction, to show where to put the book on the shelf (rough alphabetical order is enough for our purposes) and the title of the book. When kids check out a book, they just slip the card into their 'library pocket' in a wall chart of pockets and then replace the card in the book pocket before returning it to the shelf. There's another space to leave the books for people who are in a hurry. Some kids are responsible for putting the library in order from time to time. My two neighboring teachers each have wall charts of pockets in my room so that their kids can check out my books if they want.

*Field Notes: Teacher-To-Teacher*

My kinders bring in stuffed animals that they read to. I also have lots of puppet book characters that the children can use to act out the stories. I set up our class library in cubbies. Children sort books by the first letter of the author's last name.

*Janice Marshall*
*Keeling Elementary*
*Tucson, Arizona*

**Writing and Publishing Center**

Listen to what Melissa Lauren Holtzer, a second grader in Curtis Eastbrook School, Brooklyn, New York, has to say about *writer's voice*. "Voice means hearing yourself in a story. Write about something you like, so your audience will hear you in the story. Write something no one else can."

Remarkable advice from an eight year old, but then Melissa writes daily. She's a member of Maureen Powell's classroom writing community. She chooses her own writing topics from the rich material of her own life. She writes multiple drafts. She shares her writing with her peers and teacher, and uses their feedback to revise. Finally, she chooses the compositions that she deems worthy and publishes them in attractive, inviting cardboard cover books. Melissa is a writer.

## SHOPTALK

Graves, Donald. *Writing: Teachers and Children at Work*. Portsmouth, New Hampshire: Heinemann, 1983.

This may be the book that started it all, that revolutionized everything we know about writing and the teaching of writing. Graves explains the writing process and how to make it work in the classroom. He recommends that teachers write. It's much easier to work with students as writers if you understand your own writing. Graves also insists that there is practically no limit to what kids can do as writers. "At every single point in our research," he writes, "we've underestimated what kids can do."

Invite your students to become writers. Write with them and share your writing. Encourage them to write daily about topics they care about and know well. Share writing, talk writing, love writing. Your students, like Melissa, will develop as real writers. And for many helpful tips on how to support your students as writers, read Lois Bridges' *Writing as a Way of Knowing* (forthcoming).

**What to wish for**
- computer and printer (it works best if every child can have his or her own disk)
- old typewriters
- variety of writing implements
- letter templates for tracing
- variety of paper and stationery
- date stamp
- rough draft stamp (sloppy copy)
- thesauruses, dictionaries
- publishing materials of all sorts: wallpaper samples, spiral binder machine, three-hole punch, tagboard

## Making Centers Work

The writing center, art studio, science and technology center, and the many others will work when students take responsibility for making them work. Require them to control, monitor, and evaluate their own center work. Tracking forms help a lot. Here is one example. Adapt it to fit your needs.

### My Center Tracking Sheet

Name _____

Week of _____

| Centers | Date Started | Date Completed | Self-Evaluation |
|---------|--------------|----------------|-----------------|
|         |              |                |                 |
|         |              |                |                 |
|         |              |                |                 |
|         |              |                |                 |
|         |              |                |                 |
|         |              |                |                 |
|         |              |                |                 |

*The writing center, art studio, science and technology center, and the many others will work when students take responsibility for making them work.*

A final note about learning centers: Experiment! Have fun! Some centers may be permanent such as the resource center, classroom library, or listening center. Others may be portable, stored in bins or milk crates, and taken out as needed. Portable or permanent, centers are powerful pulls into learning. Let yourself be pulled.

### How To Store It

I find keeping a household of four organized is a chore. Keeping some semblance of order in a classroom of thirty is a monumental undertaking. A few tips can make a difference.

- Use clear containers to store things whenever possible; that way you and your students can see at a glance what's in the container and where to put away what's out.

- Portable coat racks make handy holders for oversized big books and chart paper.
- Alice Dalzell, a primary teacher in the Falcon School District, Peyton, Colorado, suggests storing thematic unit items in under-the-bed decorated cardboard containers found at discount stores. "Posters can be rolled and stored in these as well," Dalzell reports. "Label the side of the box and you will have easy access to your items at any time."
- Another tip from Dalzell: "Large three-ring binders adorn my teacher bookshelves. I have one labeled for every major thematic unit I teach. The binder is then divided into the major subjects. When planning learning centers, I have easy access to all disciplines."
- Bobbi Fisher of Josiah Haynes School in Sudbury, Massachusetts, keeps a recycling bag at home. Once it's full, she brings it to school and her kinders help her sort materials into labeled shoe boxes. What does she collect? Here's a short list: plastic yogurt containers, coffee scoops, pieces of string, lids, paper towel and toilet paper tubes, yarn, buttons, coffee cans, and bits of foil.

*Field Notes: Teacher-To-Teacher*

In my room, if a student has built something with blocks, it can stay up only if it has a sign instructing others to leave it alone. One day, a group of children built a big castle out of small blocks. When it was time to clean up, they covered the castle and surrounding area with at least 20 "No" signs. The castle was not to be messed with!

*Chris Boyd*
*Roadrunner School*
*Phoenix, Arizona*

**Clean-Up**

Three words on clean-up: *everybody does it*. I always gave a five-minute warning before it was time to clean up so kids could put the finishing touches on their projects, gather materials to save for the next day, or make signs for projects they didn't want disturbed. But when I put on a Raffi, Charlotte Diamond, or other favorite music tape that signaled clean-up, everyone got busy—immediately!

Chris Boyd offers these tips for making sure clean-up doesn't leave you washed up.

> Everyone cleans everything. Everyone is equal. Some children may not make much of the mess, but they still help the others that had messier projects. I am more interested in creativity during work time than cleanliness. Children can move from one project to the other and not worry about cleaning up after each thing. I don't want clean-up to inhibit work. If students have built something with Legos they take the five minutes before clean-up to draw a picture of their Lego creation. They put the picture in the Lego picture box so they can build it another day—or another student can try to replicate it. I do very little of the cleaning. I mostly help the children see things they missed and supervise the operation. Clean-up generally lasts two to five minutes if everyone is working. If I spot a child who isn't cleaning, I give that child a specific job.

---

### DIALOGUE

What's clean-up time like for me? Is it cheerful and productive? a frenetic, last minute effort? How can I make it a more pleasant, democratic process?

☐  Establish cleaning teams.

☐  Ask different children to be in charge of cleaning specific areas.

☐  Establish a rotating chart.

What suggestions do my colleagues have for keeping classrooms clean, neat, and organized?

_____

_____

---

Teacher Mary Kitagawa uses management teams to keep her room in order. "My room is divided into four teams," Mary explains. "Each week a different team has one of these tasks:

- chairs—taking down chairs from tables in the morning and putting them up before dismissal
- games and materials—restoring order to games shelf and to library
- messenger and floors—running errands anytime, checking before dismissal to be sure the vacuum cleaner can be used without interference
- distribution—passing out notices, papers, journals, and so on.

The groups are responsible as a team; when someone thinks others are shirking they are still responsible but have permission to 'nag' teammates instead of just doing it all themselves."

Clean, well-organized classrooms work best for all involved; thus all involved should be involved in clean-up. Greg Chapnick of Hayward, California, says it best: "Keeping the room clean and organized is part of the curriculum. It is everyone's responsibility, not just mine or the neat kids' or the custodian's. Clean-up is part of the activity and part of the day."

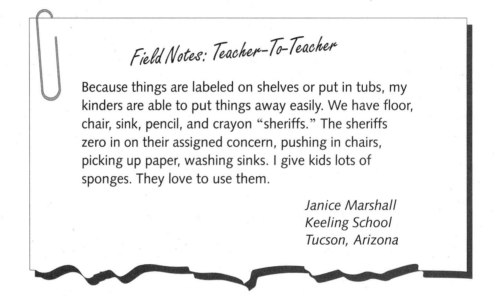

*Field Notes: Teacher-To-Teacher*

Because things are labeled on shelves or put in tubs, my kinders are able to put things away easily. We have floor, chair, sink, pencil, and crayon "sheriffs." The sheriffs zero in on their assigned concern, pushing in chairs, picking up paper, washing sinks. I give kids lots of sponges. They love to use them.

*Janice Marshall*
*Keeling School*
*Tucson, Arizona*

*In learner-centered classrooms, print is everywhere.*

### The Stuff of Learning

You know the instant you set foot in a classroom what sort of "learning life" the students are experiencing. If it's a life governed by textbooks, basal readers, and skill packs, you'll see stacks of textbooks, basal readers, skill packs, and little else. If, on the other hand, it's a life stretched and expanded in dozens of directions by real student inquiry, you'll see the rich, complex stuff of learning: discovery centers with natural wonders students have brought in; racks of student-authored stories, poetry, plays, newspapers; interdisciplinary displays—art galleries, science experiments, history and social studies dioramas; and everywhere the tools of learning—books of all sorts, fiction, reference books, magazines, maps, slides, photographs, and audio- and videotapes.

#### Print-Rich

Just as babies make sense of a world of talk, so kids will make sense of a world of print. In learner-centered classrooms, print is everywhere—real, functional print that kids need to read in order to know what time the drama club is meeting; what joke everyone is snickering about; or where to get the best deal on three-hole binder paper. New Zealand students spend time every day reading the classroom walls. (Based on per capita statistics such as magazine subscriptions, number of thriving newspapers, and bookstores, New Zealand has long enjoyed the reputation as the most literate country in the world. It's a literate tradition that begins in the classroom.) They walk around the room, interacting with the print "dripping" from the walls and ceiling. What do they read?

- labels on models kids are building
- announcements about upcoming meetings and events
- notices about lost treasures, clothes
- pictures and photographs with captions
- posters and advertisements
- lists of responsibilities, jobs
- recipes
- message center
- joke and comic board
- directions for games
- a television corner—reviews of upcoming shows, program schedules
- written explanations of student displays
- author studies—displays of their books and biographical notes about the author's life
- reports of student outings and projects
- graphs and lists (books students recommend, for example).

*Field Notes: Teacher-To-Teacher*

One of the main things we do in the fall is put up poetry on charts. We may start by copying our favorite poems from books. Or we may read aloud lots of poetry. Always, within a week, someone wants to put up his or her own poem. From then on, there is an explosion of poetry-writing, so we quickly replace the work of professional poets with our own. Soon there are poems hanging from every bit of wall space and out in the hall as well.

*Mary Kitagawa*
*Marks Meadow School*
*Amherst, Massachusetts*

## S H O P T A L K

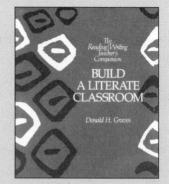

Graves, Donald. *The Reading/Writing Teacher's Companion: Build a Literate Classroom*. Portsmouth, New Hampshire: Heinemann, 1991.

Imagine that your personal library was limited to just five professional books. Which five would you select? One of my five would be *Build a Literate Classroom*. It's jam-packed with just the sort of nuts-and-bolts guidelines that teachers crave. Graves, always a pleasure to read, is clear and direct, teaching while he inspires.

Working through *Build a Literate Classroom* together as a faculty is the next best thing to having Graves on site for a year's worth of in-service. Not only will this invaluable workshop-in-a-book help you and your colleagues develop and clarify your educational philosophies, but it will guide you through the myriad decisions teachers face daily as they struggle to create literate, content-rich learning environments that will support thirty-some individual learners. Graves tackles everything from organizing the school day to teaching writing conventions, and involving students in the creation of portfolios and self-evaluation. Perhaps most important, Graves challenges readers to engage in self-reflection, the hallmark of a true professional.

## Literacy Environment Observation Sheet

Teacher _____ School _____

**Is the functional use of print for the entire classroom observed in**

☐ daily messages, schedules, assignments, notices

☐ labels (on cabinets, containers, equipment) to iden-tify needed materials and storage areas

☐ current child-written messages, labels, etc.

☐ bulletin boards related to class activities

☐ sign-up, sign-in, sign-out sheets

☐ different charts

☐ classroom rules

☐ songs

☐ nursery rhymes

☐ class or group original stories

☐ calendars

☐ class log or diary

☐ recipes

☐ project directions

☐ instructions for pet care

☐ physical arrangement of classroom and materials

**Is the functional use of print on an individual basis observable in**

☐ student labeling of own work

☐ individual journals or log books

☐ student-published materials

☐ physical and temporal access to a variety of writ-ing materials and equipment (markers, pencils, pens, chalk, paper, chalkboard, etc.)

☐ letter writing or pen pals

☐ individual messages to parents

☐ teacher notes to students

☐ opportunity and encouragement to write

**Is a variety of printed material available/accessible in**

☐ children's literature

☐ references (dictionaries, encyclopedias, charts, pictures, etc.)

☐ nonfiction information books

☐ miscellaneous print (comics, newspapers, maps, globes, student-authored books, magazines)

**Is the modeling of literacy behaviors by the teacher observable in**

☐ writing

☐ notes to parents

☐ notes to students

☐ notes to other adults

☐ notes to self

☐ classroom lists, signs, etc.

☐ revising and editing

☐ reading

☐ communicating with others

☐ reading books to children

☐ notices, announcements to kids

☐ attitudes

☐ trying new things

☐ making and pointing out own errors

☐ referring to books or other references

☐ modeling enjoyment of reading and writing

☐ responding to message over form

☐ encouraging children to attempt reading and writing

**Areas to avoid**

☐ Is there a reliance on basals and other textbooks?

☐ Is there a heavy use of ditto masters and work-books?

☐ Is there emphasis on sequential skills and "mastery?"

☐ Is there an emphasis on immediate error correction?

☐ Are all students engaged in identical activities?

**Comments:**

*The Whole Language Catalog* © 1991 edited by Kenneth S. Goodman, Lois Bridges Bird and Yetta M. Goodman, form by David Hartle-Shutte

## S H O P T A L K

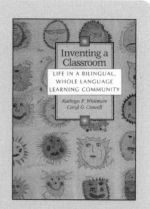

Whitmore, Kathryn F. and Caryl G. Crowell. *Inventing a Classroom. Life in a Bilingual, Whole Language Learning Community.* York, Maine: Stenhouse Publishers, 1994.

Whitmore, an ethnographer and teacher educator, and Crowell, a talented classroom teacher, together tell the story of the Sunshine Room, Crowell's bicultural third grade classroom in a bilingual, working class neighborhood. What does it mean to invent a classroom? What are the implications for teaching? for curriculum? for assessment? community? literacy? Readers will find answers to these questions and more, and, in the process, learn how to consciously invent their own classrooms in ways that support children as competent, creative learners.

*Chapter 4*

# The Learning Life

How should we define schooling? I like John Dewey's answer: "School is not preparation for life, it is life." When school is viewed as life, as a place to stimulate and nurture deep thoughtfulness and creative exploration, immediate changes take place that impact the teacher's role, the student's role, and what gets taught. All undergo a dramatic transformation. Let's explore.

## *What the Teacher Does*

It's not possible to list what teachers really do. No list could capture the myriad decisions and moves you make nearly every minute of every school day. But for purposes of discussion, I'd like to identify three major teaching-learning responsibilities.

- Teachers immerse students in rich learning.
- Teachers demonstrate effective learning.
- Teachers teach responsively.

**Teachers immerse students in rich learning.** Almost from the day of birth, children have innumerable opportunities to use oral language to meet their needs and desires. We teach them how to live in our homes and in our communities, and we use language to do much of the teaching. Children are immersed in rich, functional language from the moment they rise in the morning until they tumble into bed at night. In the process, they learn what language is and how it works.

The concept of immersion is key in understanding how learner-centered classrooms work. Just as children are immersed in rich oral language at home, so we want to immerse them in content-rich, literate environments at school. To fully awaken our students' learning energies, we need to surround them with the riveting stuff of learning: print materials of all sorts, hands-on artifacts, maps, photographs, diagrams, art, and discovery centers. A learner-centered classroom is organized but full of student projects and investigations. Every available bit of space is taken up with student inquiries across the curriculum.

Kittye Copeland, a multigrade teacher in Stephens Elementary School in Columbia, Missouri, explains how she immerses her students in a content-rich, literate classroom learning environment.

*To fully awaken our students' learning energies, we need to surround them with the riveting stuff of learning: print materials of all sorts, hands-on artifacts, maps, photographs, diagrams, art, and discovery centers.*

At the beginning of the year, I send a letter home inviting my students to bring posters, animals, plants, books, magazines, brochures, and decorations to help make the classroom a student-owned environment. I want them to know that our room is their "living space" as well as mine. When my students arrive, they help me arrange furniture and set up areas that will help us function as a learning community. We create reading areas, writing labs, literature discussion areas, experimentation centers, large- and small-group meeting areas, game areas, listening centers, and research areas. I also establish mailboxes for each learner and we set up a classroom post office. In addition, we create a message board and a class magazine. There is a lot of communicating in our classroom—and a lot to do.

*Field Notes: Teacher-To-Teacher*

Supplies are always out in an accessible place for the children so they don't need to depend on me to get them out. Glue, staplers, scissors, paper of many sizes (especially recycled project papers), pencils, material scraps, recycled cardboard and plastic containers, paper and paper towel tubes, water paint, tempera paint, sponges, brushes of several sizes, hot trays for melted crayon pictures, paper clips, brads, tape—it's all out on the shelves, always ready to be used.

*Chris Boyd*
*Roadrunner School*
*Phoenix, Arizona*

## SHOPTALK

Duckworth, Eleanor. *The Having of Wonderful Ideas and Other Essays on Teaching and Learning.* New York: Teachers College Press, 1987.

Sandra Wilde of Portland State University talks about Duckworth's book. "This may be one of the best books about teaching and learning ever written. In a variety of fascinating essays about such topics as children making bulbs light up and teachers observing the moon and thinking about what they see, Duckworth offers a distinctly Piagetian perspective on how we come to know, and on the role schools play in that knowing. Duckworth combines a strong background in Piaget (she worked with him and was one of his translators) with a probing intelligence that is never content to take things for granted. Every page contains interesting revelations and insights. The main message to a reader of this book is that it is absolutely imperative for learners to reinvent the wheel, for it is through invention rather than transmission that true learning occurs."

**Teachers demonstrate effective learning.** In 1988, I heard Shirley Brice Heath speak at a National Council of Teachers of English conference about the importance of providing students with models of "joyful literacy." She said that sometimes, if only one person in a child's life demonstrates what it means to be a joyfully aware, joyfully involved, literate person, that will help the child become literate as well. Not surprisingly, then, in autobiographical essays, famous writers frequently describe a family member who demonstrated daily the joys of reading. The family member not only read, but talked about the reading as well, pointing out and discussing favorite passages. Through these literate demonstrations, the writer, as a child, came to understand and love the rhythmical patterns of written language, growing up to control those patterns in his or her own writing.

We often learn best through apprenticeship, by watching someone do something that we want to do. Classrooms should be places where children can see the strategies of successful learning demonstrated daily. Teachers should show their students what it means to be an effective learner. The best place to begin is for teachers to share their "learning lives" with their students. As often as possible, teachers should demonstrate all the different ways in which it's possible to learn about the world through language, the visual and performing arts, math, and science.

Demonstrations show children how something *might* be done—not how it *must* be done. When we demonstrate our love of reading by reading our own books in class, by talking about the books we are reading, and by writing about them in a literature log, we don't insist that our students respond to their books in exactly the same way. Rather, we know that as we share the complexities of our reading lives, our students will learn about the joy and satisfaction of being a reader and what to anticipate as they embark on their own reading lives.

Leslie Mangiola, an upper elementary teacher at Fair Oaks School in Redwood City, California, shows her students how she works to find answers to her questions, and how she uses a variety of learning strategies and tools. Leslie explains: "I'll often start off the school day by posting a real question that I'm grappling with. For example, right now I'm faced with buying a new car. So I wrote on the board, "What is the best car for me for the money?" I then told my students how much money I had to work with, and how I was trying to find answers to that question. Almost every day, I would report on my progress. I told my kids how I sought out the advice of friends whose opinions about cars I respected. I read *Road and Track* magazine and *Consumer Reports*, and I talked with different sales people and actually test drove several cars. In this way, I demonstrated to my kids how people rely on multiple resources to help them learn. Contrary to what a lot of kids grow up thinking, an encyclopedia is only one way to access information.

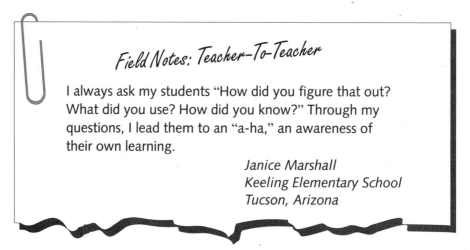

*Field Notes: Teacher-To-Teacher*

I always ask my students "How did you figure that out? What did you use? How did you know?" Through my questions, I lead them to an "a-ha," an awareness of their own learning.

*Janice Marshall*
*Keeling Elementary School*
*Tucson, Arizona*

In a similar way, Kittye Copeland shows her students in Stephens Elementary, Columbia, Missouri, the process she follows as a writer. "I am not just a person there to teach them but to share my use and value of language," explains Copeland. "Many times as I write, I seek help from my students. I ask them for revision suggestions or editing needs. It is not a set-up situation, I really want their advice and the students know it. Students must see their teachers' efforts when writing as well as their written products. They need to observe teachers as they write, to see all that is involved when engaged in writing. The times students spend observing and interacting with their teachers in the role of writers is an enormous benefit in their understanding of writing.

*Field Notes: Teacher-To-Teacher*

We talk about what a good learner looks like and what a good listener does. With kindergartners, it takes a while, but they begin to internalize our discussions. We do a lot of role-playing, and I participate and demonstrate effective listening and learning, too.

The best way to assess whether children truly know something is for them to teach others.

*Janice Marshall*
*Keeling Elementary*
*Tucson, Arizona*

*Good teaching, like good writing, is created and crafted through a continuous process of revision.*

**Teachers teach responsively.** In learner-centered classrooms, teachers don't take their instructional cues from basal readers or textbooks. What to do Monday morning isn't found on page 24 of the teacher's manual. Teachers, as professional educators, decide what to teach. As they develop their teaching plans, they draw from three sources:

- theoretical understanding of learning and how best to support learning in the classroom
- instructional vision (often influenced by state and district curricular guidelines)
- kidwatching data; awareness of their students' strengths and needs.

Good teaching, like good writing, is created and crafted through a continuous process of revision. The teacher, like the writer, asks: What is working? What isn't working? What do I have to rework, and how should I go about it? Such questions lead to changes, to appraisal of the results, and to further revision.

This is responsive teaching. Donald Murray, professor emeritus of the University of New Hampshire and Donald Graves' mentor, says the most effective teaching is responsive. Frank Smith (1983) instructs us, simply, "Respond to what the child is trying to do."

We can respond to our students in sensitive and supportive ways when we engage in kidwatching—observing students carefully as they go about their learning. Once we've completed our observations, we need to take a moment to step outside of the rush of classroom activity and reflect on, interpret, and learn from our kidwatching. This "debriefing" process is critical to effective, responsive teaching. *Assessment: Continuous Learning* (1995) provides more information on kidwatching.

## SHOPTALK

Calkins, Lucy McCormick. *The Art of Teaching Writing.* New Edition. Portsmouth, New Hampshire, 1994.

Effective teaching, like effective writing, generally demands rethinking and revising. Not surprisingly, then, the 1994 edition of the original 1986 *The Art of Teaching Writing* is less a second edition than a whole new book. Lucy Calkins has rethought "every line and facet of her original text." While the content has changed, Calkins' gift for storytelling has not. A substantial 550 pages, the book, is nonetheless, an easy, inspiring read. And like the original, the new edition teaches as it inspires. Teachers from preschool to high school will discover how to learn from children what to teach, how to create a viable writing workshop that supports students across the developmental continuum, how to explore multiple genres, and how to use writing to learn about the world.

My 1986 edition is tattered from use; the 1994 edition will grow old before its time for the same reason—Calkins is a masterful, compassionate teacher of writing.

See also *Living Between the Lines* (1990). Calkins and Shelly Harwayne's recommendations are simple: Narrow the gap between what professional writers do and what we expect kids to do in schools. You'll become convinced of the value of inviting students to keep writing notebooks and will want to start keeping one yourself.

Greg Chapnick considers kidwatching critical for effective teaching. Indeed, without careful observation of his students in all areas, academic as well as social and personal, he says he wouldn't know how to go about his teaching work. "If you don't pay attention to what the kids are saying and especially to what they are doing," Chapnick reports, "you are going to have a rough time. Watching them over time—kidwatching—is the most valuable tool of our teaching trade."

Kidwatching isn't incidental to good teaching, it's essential. Good kidwatchers are good teachers. Good kidwatchers come to know their students, understand well their strengths and needs, know when to step in and nudge, or when to pull back and let children take the lead. Good kidwatchers learn what questions to ask and when. Good kidwatchers discover how to make informed decisions about what to teach and when to teach it. But kidwatching, like every other ability in the world, is learned through practice, through experimentation, self-reflection, more practice, and revision. And the best time to begin is now—in your own classroom with your own students.

---

### DIALOGUE

To help you debrief—to reflect on and interpret—the living and learning you and your students experience within your classroom learning community, try answering the questions from the Teacher Self-Reflection form. The form signals a "time out," a chance to catch your breath and reflect on your kidwatching, to determine what has been working for you and your students, what hasn't been working as well, and how you might go about revising your teaching.

#### Teacher Self-Reflection

What worked for me as the teacher? What didn't? Why? (Consider time, resources, materials, learning modalities, disciplines.)

_____

What worked for the students? What didn't? Why? (Consider time, resources, materials, learning modalities, disciplines.)

_____

What strengths and needs did I notice in my students?

_____

How will I use this information to plan my next instructional steps?

_____

Make as many copies of the form as you need and use them at any point in the school day as you feel a need to breathe, reflect, learn, and revise your teaching. In this way, you'll develop and refine your teaching art.

## S H O P T A L K

Barr, Mary. *The California Learning Record*. Sacramento: California State Department of Education, 1993.

Adapted from the British *Primary Language Record*, this remarkable document encourages and shows teachers how to identify children's strengths and note growth points, how to regard errors as information, and how to analyze patterns of error in constructive ways. For those committed to authentic assessment—classroom-based teacher observation and anecdotal record-keeping—this is an evaluation tool you'll not want to be without.

### What the Students Do

Students stay busy in classrooms. They may not be busy doing what we want them to do, but kids are generally good at keeping themselves engaged and occupied with something. In a classroom community, students stay busy by

- taking risks
- making choices
- working together
- controlling, monitoring, and evaluating their own learning.

**Students take risks.** I used to teach downhill skiing to six year olds. Two or three times out on skis, and the kids were flying down hills that only the most experienced adult would attempt. How did my six year olds learn to ski so quickly? They took risks. I don't mean to suggest that they risked breaking their necks (although their parents might disagree). I do mean that they weren't afraid to try skiing in any way they could, which meant that they often fell down. But they'd get up and try again, following in my trail as best they could as I led the way down the mountain. Unlike most adult beginning skiers, they weren't afraid to fall. They took the risks necessary to learn.

The first few times we try something—skiing, bike riding, reading a book—we make mistakes; we fall down a lot. But if we keep trying to follow our teacher down the mountain, around the block, or through a book, before too long, we're skiing, bike riding, or reading on our own. Playing it safe and being overly concerned with correctness stifles learning. Teachers need to trust that their students' approximations are signs of growth, indices of real learning. Their first time out on the slope, my little skiers managed their skis in any way they could. When they fell, I pulled them up, brushed the snow off their backsides, and sent them down the slope again, cheering whether they were upright or not. They kept working, and it wasn't long before I had to work to keep up with them! When we support and celebrate our students' efforts, they will take the risks necessary to learn.

*Field Notes: Teacher-To-Teacher*

My expectation is that students try, that they make as strong an effort as possible in whatever area we are working. I stress the value of "mistakes" and risk-taking as means to eventual success. To promote this, I attempt to create learning situations where more than one right answer is always possible. I also tell kids over and over that the way I can best tell how well they are learning is by the questions they ask and the "mistakes" they make. I make sure that they understand why and how I value "mistakes" and why I put quotes around the word.

*Greg Chapnick*
*Charquin School*
*Hayward, California*

*When we support and celebrate our students' efforts, they will take the risks necessary to learn.*

**Students make choices.** I have several friends who are taking adult education classes. One friend is enrolled in a life-drawing class; another, in a writing class; and still another is taking a course on body sculpting. All three friends are passionately interested in their chosen subjects. They look forward to attending their classes, and talk enthusiastically about what they are learning. As adults, we have the luxury of choosing what we want to learn. But choice shouldn't be reserved only for adults.

It is simply true that it is easier to learn about those things that you are interested in and care about. When you allow your students real choices—which books they will read, what drawings they will include in their portfolios, how they will share their science experiments—you enable your students to take ownership of their learning. And with ownership comes commitment and levels of productive engagement rarely achieved with teacher-given assignments. "From observations outside of school," writes Gordon Wells (1986), "we know that students are innately predisposed to make sense of their experience, to pose problems for themselves, and actively to search for and achieve solutions. They will continue to bring these characteristics to bear inside the school as well, provided that the tasks they engage in are ones they have been able to make their own."

Giving students choice doesn't mean that you give up your say in what gets done, or when. There are ways to combine the best of both. Martha Ahlman, a primary, multigrade teacher in Chuska School, Tohatchi, New Mexico, uses a "Plan-Do-Review" strategy. It fosters choice and self-responsibility, and, Ahlman reports, "The children love it, and so do I and my instructional aide. During this time, the children decide and plan what they want to do from among the choices in the room. They either write it down or sign up. Older ones can estimate how long they think it will take. Then, after the time is up, they review what they did. Was it successful? Do they need to work on it some more? Our children choose painting, puppets, sewing, reading, writing, science experiments, listening, computers, or math manipulatives. This is usually the quietest time of the day for us!"

*Field Notes: Teacher-To-Teacher*

Kids have many decisions to make in my classroom. The only decision that is never okay is a decision *not* to make a decision!

Mary Kitagawa
Marks Meadow School
Amherst, Massachusetts

In a similar way, Judy Bloomington-Vinke, a language arts resource teacher at Mitchell Elementary School in Lawndale, California, offers her students choice within a clearly defined structure. She explains, "I find that the formula, *Yours, Mine, and Ours*, provides us with a comfortable balance of student choice and teacher control. *Yours* refers to the choices my students make; *Mine* is reserved for the things I'd like them to do; and *Ours* is a choice negotiated by us both. For example, in reading workshop, I invite my students to choose a book they'd like to read (Yours). They must also read one from the district reading list (Mine). Together, we select several books the whole class will read by the year's end (Ours)."

*Field Notes: Teacher-To-Teacher*

I offer limited choice. I use an analogy of a path. In overly structured classes, the path is very narrow and defined. You know exactly where to go and when because there are no choices. My path is a little wider. There is more than one way to get to where you are going. As the year progresses, the path widens or branches so that the possibilities and choices increase.

*Greg Chapnick*
*Charquin School*
*Hayward, California*

*In an effective classroom community, everyone is alternately a teacher and a learner.*

**Students work together.** Learning is a social activity. Three or four students working together will almost certainly produce more productive results than just one working alone. Students learn from each other—skills, strategies, content information. What one doesn't know, another likely will. In an effective classroom community, everyone is alternately a teacher and a learner. Teachers foster in all their students a sense that they know things that they can teach to others. Following the lead of Donald Graves (1983), many teachers strive to help every child carve out his or her own area of expertise. Some teachers like to post an "Experts List" in their classrooms, identifying each student with their area of expertise. Rosa is a spelling whiz; Gabriel knows everything there is to know about raising rabbits; Curtis is the one to see if you need help with math. Once the list is up, it is used daily. This means that students depend on their peers for assistance; asking the teacher for help is just one option.

When one of her students shares a problem, primary teacher Chris Boyd asks the class who will volunteer to help the child and serve as a learning partner in the future. Eventually, the children can identify on their own who to see for specific problems. In fact, Boyd writes, "When the call goes out for a specific expert, classmates will recommend other classmates whom they know possess the needed skill or talent."

Mary Kitagawa reports that her students name strategies after the child from whom they learned it. Mary is delighted when she hears, "I did it Tobin's way," or "I did what Leah did." "I'm never sure where this comes from," says Kitagawa, "but maybe it happens when talk is a big part of the classroom."

Martha Ahlman finds that her multigrade classroom naturally fosters cooperation and collaboration.

> We have a multiage group of Navajo children, ranging in age from five and a half to nine years old and first to fourth grade. The children stay with the class for four years. In our class, we have two brother-sister combinations. The brothers are both in the first grade and the sisters are both in third grade. By its very nature, the classroom instills within the children a sense of responsibility. The older children both help the younger ones and serve as role models. There is constant interaction between ages. We are set up more like a family group than a traditional one-age classroom, and the children respond to this expectation.

Greg Chapnick, who also teaches in a multigrade classroom, finds that when he stresses his own learning in the classroom, his students begin to appreciate themselves and each other as learners.

> I stress that I am a learner, too. Whenever I learn a new fact or idea from a child (which happens frequently), I celebrate it. This year I learned something from a boy who has great difficulty focusing on his work. He is very bright, but easily distracted. We were talking about even and odd numbers. I grew up learning that even numbers were 2, 4, 6, 8, etc., and odds were 1, 3, 5, 7, etc., but I don't think I could tell you much more. This student pointed out that if you drew dots to represent each number and paired off the dots in two columns, each dot of an even number had a "partner"— they were evenly matched, while odd numbers always had one dot left over—not evenly matched. One of those simple truths, but I never thought about it that way. So, not only did I learn, but I took the opportunity to present this child, who experiences few moments of success, as a brilliant scholar and teacher.

*Field Notes: Teacher-To-Teacher*

I encourage my students to establish their own classroom rules, but there is one rule I give them the first week of school: "Ask three before you ask me." I want them to view each other not just as classmates, but as helpmates. This rule helps us to establish a collaborative learning family where everyone, including me, is both a teacher and a learner.

*Rena Malkofsky*
*El Carmelo School*
*Palo Alto, California*

Crafton, Linda. *Whole Language: Getting Started...Moving Forward.* Katonah, New York: Richard C. Owen, 1991.

Wendy Hood from Warren Elementary School in Tucson, Arizona says, "The more I read and reread *Whole Language: Getting Started... Moving Forward,* the more excited I become. Skillfully, like a good teacher, Linda Crafton guides the reader through a process of self-evaluation. Each chapter in Part I presents a balance of learner-centered theory supported by classroom vignettes, ending with suggested issues for 'personal reflection.' Part II develops learner-centered strategies. The learner-centered principles outlined in Chapter 1 are not merely mentioned, they are present throughout the content and format of the book."

Initially, Leslie Mangiola, at Fair Oaks School in Redwood City, California, groups her students to create an effective mix of talents and interests, balancing strengths and weaknesses. But she finds that eventually her students can form their own groups, coming together around their common interests. Mangiola and her fifth graders have frequent class discussions about what it means to be a good partner and how to cooperate and work collaboratively. Their discussions go a long way in helping assure the success of their small group work. In addition, Mangiola often asks the children to evaluate the success of their group work once they've completed a project. She provides a simple form which they fill in.

- I felt that our group worked well together because...
- Next time we can be more effective if we...

Mangiola's students learn what it means to cooperate and collaborate with their peers. She reports that "they feel great when they can see how their ideas and input have helped others to learn."

**Students control, monitor, and evaluate their own learning.** There are those like Courtney Cazden of the Harvard University School of Education, who believe that the very essence of education is the ability to step back from your learning and examine it—what is working for me? What isn't working as well? What can I do to become a more effective learner? *Metacognition,* or turning thought in on itself, is the official term for this self-reflection. But whatever we choose to call it, the results are the same: students become thoughtful, confident learners who have a sense of their own questions, who understand how to find the resources needed to answer their questions, and who know when, why, and how their own learning is working for them. With this awareness comes power—the ability to control and shape their own learning destiny.

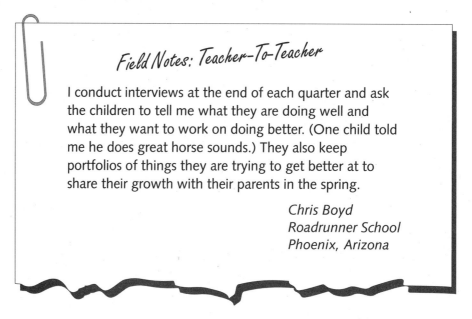

*Field Notes: Teacher-To-Teacher*

I conduct interviews at the end of each quarter and ask the children to tell me what they are doing well and what they want to work on doing better. (One child told me he does great horse sounds.) They also keep portfolios of things they are trying to get better at to share their growth with their parents in the spring.

*Chris Boyd*
*Roadrunner School*
*Phoenix, Arizona*

Alyce Dalzell teaches third graders at Falcon Elementary School in Peyton, Colorado. She invites her students to complete daily and weekly self-evaluation forms. She finds that her students "assume responsibility" and "take ownership of their learning by setting realistic goals." Dalzell notes that "children are empowered by completing self-evaluations of their work."

---

**Daily Self-Evaluation**

Name_____ Date_____

My goal for the day is _____

_____

I will help myself reach my goal by _____

_____

To reach my goal, I need help from _____

_____

Today I _____

_____

## Weekly Self-Evaluation

Name _____ Date _____

This week I learned _____

_____

_____

What was most important to me this week was _____

_____

_____

I did very well _____

_____

_____

I am confused about _____

_____

_____

I still need to work on _____

_____

_____

Student signature _____

Teacher signature _____

Parent signature _____

In Kittye Copeland's K-6 classroom, students work in small group research teams. Once they've completed their research, they think of a way to share it with their peers. After the presentation, the audience completes this form.

**Student Evaluation of Peer Reports**

Name _____ Date _____

Evaluation of _____ Report

Topic _____

What I liked best _____

_____

What I think would have improved the report _____

_____

I learned _____

_____

I would like to learn _____

_____

Teacher Martha Ahlmann relies on portfolios to encourage student self-evaluation. The children choose the work that goes into their portfolios. They look through their portfolios periodically to evaluate their progress. For example, they might look at their writing and consider: How has my writing changed from the beginning of the year? What can I do now that I couldn't do before?

**DIALOGUE**

In what ways do I foster student self-evaluation?

☐ reflective learning logs      ☐ self-evaluation forms

☐ learning portfolios          ☐ reflective discussions

☐ other ways _____

How might I increase opportunities for student self-reflection and evaluation?

_____

Greg Chapnick has his students write to help reflect on their learning.

> I always encourage informal self-evaluation over teacher evaluation. In math and science, I often have my students write about their problem solving. It is the hardest kind of writing for them. It comes very slowly, but often they have the most fun with it. Partly it involves writing clear descriptions, but the other part of it involves reflecting on their own problem-solving process. The next thing I'd like to do is help the kids develop rubrics for evaluating their own work.

## SHOPTALK

Goodman, Kenneth S., Yetta M. Goodman and Wendy J. Hood. *The Whole Language Evaluation Book*. Portsmouth, New Hampshire: Heinemann, 1988.

This was one of the first books to address the whys, whats and hows of authentic assessment. The book is chock full of evaluation forms and strategies developed by experienced whole language teachers. The book covers evaluation from kindergarten to high school and addresses the challenges of second language learners, and the concerns of teachers, administrators, and parents who are exploring authentic assessment.

*Student inquiry can be a powerful way to organize our curriculum.*

## What Gets Taught?

Students have big questions about the world: How does the moon turn? Why do people kill endangered animals? Why does oil float on rainwater and make rainbows? Our students' questions are worthy of our respect and support, and can become the stuff of engaging classroom inquiry. Inquiry, in fact, becomes a powerful way to organize our curriculum.

How do we find out what our students are interested in? Often all we need to do is ask them, "What have you always wondered about?" I've asked this question of students a lot, and, together, we have never failed to generate a long list of possible research topics—everything from bats to biospheres. In Columbia, Missouri, Robin Meyers tells her seventh graders, "This is your seventh-grade English class. What do you want to learn this year?" Her students' initial puzzled resistance gives way to passionate discussion as they realize she is serious about balancing her instructional agenda with their needs, concerns, and interests. Together they negotiate a curriculum that addresses the state and district curriculum frameworks, while also incorporating topics students care about.

Chris Boyd taps the interests of her kindergartners in yet another way. At the beginning of each year she makes home visits and asks the children what they want to study. She makes a list for each child and refers to it as she plans instruction and curriculum. She also adds to the lists as children mention other interests during the year. "Their interests become long-term studies or short mini-lessons," Boyd explains. "Or I give something else we are studying a different slant in order to incorporate a child's interest."

Rise Paynter, in Geneseo, New York, gives her fifth graders a "Wonderful Questions" Journal. It's eight pages long. Each page lists two questions.

1. (Student's question)
2. Why is this important to me?

The children are encouraged to think of all their important questions and record them within a week's time. They spend another week sharing their journals with each other. As a result of the sharing, the kids form Explorer Clubs around shared questions. They then work together to research, collate, and share the answers to their questions with others before forming new Explorer Clubs to research new questions.

### The Tools of Learning

In inquiry classrooms, the separate disciplines are important, but rather than serving as the "masters of the curriculum," they become "curricular servants" (Harste 1993). Language, literature, social studies, dance, art, music, drama, math, and science are areas of study in their own right. But equally important, and perhaps more so for students embarking on their quest to understand the world, they are learning tools. In an inquiry-driven curriculum, students use the content areas and a range of learning modalities to answer their questions and extend their understandings.

When I taught first grade I organized my curriculum around themes to integrate my instruction. I didn't teach content areas as separate subjects; rather, I presented them as interdisciplinary tools that helped my students define and understand a chosen theme. One year our curriculum was organized around a theme of "change." We followed the changes in ourselves—charting our physical growth as well as our social and academic spurts. We charted weather and seasonal changes. We investigated chemical changes in cooking. We charted demographic change in our community. We also looked at how Maurice Sendak's style as an author and illustrator changed over time, and monitored and documented the developmental changes in ourselves as authors. In this way, change was our focus, not the separate content areas. My students developed their intellectual tools—writing, reading, math, science, social studies, art, music, dance, drama—as they used them to relate their new insights and understandings. Organizing my curriculum around a theme helped my kids make the learning connections that lead to thoughtful conceptual understanding.

Multigrade teacher, Martha Ahlman, works with her elementary-age students for four years. To meet their curricular needs, she rotates them through four basic themes. All curriculum content is integrated around the theme. For example, when the students study the rainforest, they learn about mapping, early explorers, ships, and the sink/float concept. They establish a timeline so that they can discover how early American cultures compare in time with the early cultures of the rainforest. Martha also ties in literature so the children read jungle stories and biographies of Pocahontas and William Bradford. They write about what they read. They graph their favorite characters, and they create "talking" murals about their favorite stories. They also relate their artwork to their reading, and write math story problems that stem from their literature books.

Beside personal interests and the disciplines, Jerome Harste (1993) recommends that we also consider the sign systems—other forms of expression, alternative ways of knowing and composing.

When we think of composing, we most often think of the writing process, which may include such component aspects as prewriting, drafting, revising, conferring, and editing. However, when we extend that model beyond writing to other forms of expression, we discover that the thinking processes involved are very much the same. Whether children are composing through art, music, drama, movement, or writing, they are involved in

- generating ideas
- drafting or trying out their ideas
- conferring with others
- revising and polishing
- presenting to others what they have learned and created.

Building on Howard Gardner's theory of multiple intelligences, Dorothy Strickland (1991) asks that we consider a "communicative data pool" that includes alternative ways of creating and sharing meaning. "Research suggests that children use many different communication systems," writes Strickland, "to construct meaning for themselves and to convey what they know to others."

## Field Notes: Teacher-To-Teacher

When we were studying the sun, the children were very interested in how it worked and had an argument about where the fire came from. It's not the kind of thing I thought they could find out experimentally so we did a movement activity. The children grouped themselves like hydrogen molecule electrons and squished up to another hydrogen molecule. They smashed to the floor to become liquid, and then floated off in different groups as they exploded into helium gas. The children don't understand nuclear fusion from this activity. But, they do feel a sense of understanding, that will help them piece things together later.

*Chris Boyd*
*Roadrunner School*
*Phoenix, Arizona*

In Phoenix, Arizona, at Awakening Seed School, Yvonne Mersereau worked to help her students understand the importance of writer's voice using dance as a tool. She involved her students in a month-long author's study of Maurice Sendak. They interpreted his stories *Where the Wild Things Are, In the Night*

*Kitchen,* and *Outside Over There,* in dance. Later, they tried to represent William Steig's *Sylvester and the Magic Pebble* in dance. "They found that the specificity of Steig's language hindered them from interpreting it in dance," writes Mersereau. "Sendak's more open and abstract language allowed them more freedom of interpretation." Suddenly the cadences of Sendak's voice come alive for the children. Through dance, they came to understand in a profound way the persona of the writer's voice (Mersereau, Glover, and Cherland 1991).

## SHOPTALK

Short, Kathy G., Jerome C. Harste with Carolyn Burke. *Creating Classrooms for Authors and Inquirers.* 2d ed. Portsmouth, New Hampshire: Heinemann, 1995.

Fans of the first edition (and there are many) may notice that the second edition now includes *Inquirers* in the title. That's because, as the authors explain, they've reconceptualized everything—reading, writing, teaching, assessment, and curriculum—around inquiry. Indeed, the authors no longer pose as experts themselves but as honest inquirers who continue to question, rethink and revise, and who invite their audience to do the same. This is a ground-breaking professional book—a provocative treatise on curriculum as inquiry, an invitation to classroom research, and a nuts and bolts guide to practical instructional strategies.

Pam Adair teaches second and third graders at Fair Oaks School, in Redwood City, California, an inner city school that is 95 percent Latino. Many Fair Oaks students have just arrived from Mexico or Central America and speak only their primary language, Spanish.

Adair gives her students many ways to discover meaning and to share what they've learned with others. By providing lots of nonverbal ways to access information, she involves them in all the projects in which her English-speaking children are engaged. When the class embarked on a month-long study of Martin Luther King, Jr. and civil rights, Adair showed them the video *Eyes on the Prize,* a documentary about the Civil Rights movement. She brought in old *Life* magazines with vivid black and white pictures of scenes from the Civil Rights movement, and they listened to audiotapes of songs like "We Shall Overcome." A teacher in the school who had been active in the movement talked with Adair's students about his experiences. They also read and discussed, in English and Spanish, fiction books and biographies about King and Rosa Parks. Adair read aloud parts of Walter Dean Myers' book, *Now Is Your Time: The African-American Struggle for Freedom*. At the end of the study, working in small groups, the children dramatized different aspects of their study. The Spanish speakers achieved a sensitive understanding of the issues surrounding civil rights in this country through their access to alternative modes of communication: visual images in video, photographs and illustrations, music, movement, and drama.

### Theme Cycles

A "theme cycle" is a simple yet effective way to create and support an inquiry curriculum. It follows a six-step process.

**1. How to choose an inquiry topic.** You can find a topic in a number of ways.

- Your choice. Tell the kids that together you are going to explore a topic that you have selected.
- Student choice. Choose a topic from a student-generated list of questions in response to the questions, "What have you always wondered about? What interests you?"
- State- or district-mandated curriculum. In California, for example, fourth grade social studies is devoted to state history. Within that framework, you can find a topic or several that students can research within the structure of a theme cycle.
- Textbook. Let kids identify and research questions in their textbooks that they find interesting.
- Compelling issue. Sometimes an issue or concern will arise, sparked by a specific incident or a literature book. These current issues and events are also a rich source for student inquiry.

**2. What we know.** Invite students to brainstorm everything they know about the topic. In this way, they establish their knowledge base. You'll see what they already know about the topic and what interests them the most about it. Try semantic webs or charts to capture and organize the information generated by the brainstorm.

**3. What we want to find out.** Once children have identified what they do know about the chosen topic, they turn their attention next to what they don't know and what they want to find out. What questions do they have regarding the topic? The questions children generate become the focal point of inquiry. Students divide themselves into smaller groups around the question or questions they wish to explore. In other words, within the overarching theme, students work in small groups researching related questions.

**4. How we can find information.** The fourth step of the theme cycle entails identifying and locating research materials. Students reexamine their questions and think about how and where they can find answers. With teacher-assigned research reports, students rarely venture beyond an encyclopedia for information. With a theme cycle, students function just like real researchers and use a wide range of materials and human resources. Actual researchers spend time in the library and read everything they can get their hands on related to their topic, including newspapers, magazines, and journals from historical archives. But they also talk to people who might know something. Real researchers interview, conduct surveys, spend time observing the phenomenon they are researching, and, depending on the nature of the topic, conduct a variety of experiments. There are a lot of ways to find out about things. Researchers use them all. They include

- print materials of all sorts, fiction and nonfiction
- media—films, video and audiotapes, laserdiscs, software
- hands-on artifacts
- community, local experts
- the greater community—contacted by mail, telephone, Internet.

**5. How to research: finding answers.** Conducting effective research requires specific skills and strategies. In order to make sure our students are prepared to engage in research, we should take time each day to demonstrate a specific research technique. Some teachers find it helpful to take their students through a theme cycle as a whole class—working together to develop needed research strategies—before students engage in their own independent projects. Research tools you may want to familiarize your students with include

- how to use multiple resources
- skimming
- note-taking
- conducting interviews and surveys, writing questionnaires
- observing
- comparing, categorizing, classifying
- learning logs.

**6. How to share the findings.** We bring the process of learning to a complete circle when we have the opportunity to share with others what we have learned and, also, to reflect on the experience ourselves. We shape, refine, and extend our learning. The best way to learn, in fact, is to teach. And the best way to share your research? It depends on the nature of your data. Students should have a wide variety of presentational formats from which to choose.

These formats can include

- letters to the editor
- poster sessions, bulletin boards
- scrapbook or photo album
- oral histories and interviews
- class newspaper
- surveys, interviews, questionnaires
- slide or video presentation
- debate or panel discussion
- models and maps
- diagrams, tables, graphs, flowcharts, timelines
- role-playing, socio-drama
- art, song, dance, food
- museum kits.

They will need to carefully consider the nature of their data, and design a format that will best showcase it.

**Designing and launching a theme cycle.** Just as there is no one right way to involve students in theme cycles, so there is no one right way to launch a cycle. There are many entry points, and often, they are integrated and over-lapping, working together to highlight the possibility of further learning.

Let's see how Beth Huntzinger launched and designed a theme cycle with her kindergartners at Columbia Community School in Sunnyvale, California. As we examine Huntzinger's experience, you'll see how her students drew from multiple disciplines and skills to re-search their chosen topic. They naturally used reading and language arts, math, science, and social studies as well as all the accompanying problem-solving skills: reading, writing, calculating, measuring, estimating, drawing conclusions, and so forth. Spurred on by the need and desire to understand their topic, these young children engaged easily and naturally in interdisciplinary exploration.

## Field Notes: Teacher-To-Teacher

A student-generated theme cycle (instead of a teacher-generated thematic unit) is the most powerful idea I am currently working with. We have to study early U.S. history, but I open it up to my students' questions. What about the topic interests them? We started with what the children knew or thought they knew about U.S. history. Then we moved on to questions that they had or that came up as they brainstormed their knowledge. We talked, voted, and talked some more. "Thinking this way is hard," they complained. I agreed and we continued. The next discussion was a lot easier for them. We are reorganizing our questions, looking for resources, and deciding what activities we should try.

*Greg Chapnick*
*Charquin School*
*Hayward, California*

Huntzinger planned a theme cycle based on the guidelines of the California State Department of Education's History-Social Science Framework which, at the kindergarten level, calls for an exploration of times past. She believed that the best way to learn about life long ago was to see that world through the eyes of those who had lived it—the children's own grandparents and elderly friends and relatives.

Huntzinger introduced her theme cycle with literature, using "text sets," an instructional strategy that highlights learning as a social and cognitive process of making connections. When readers read two or more texts that are related in some way, they are encouraged to share and extend their understanding of each text differently than if they had discussed only one text. Learning and understanding is a process of searching for and making connections. We can understand what we read because of the connections we make between our current reading and our past experiences. Text sets comprise a variety of written materials that are related in some way. We invite our students to read from different sources within that set, and come together in discussion groups to share and make comparisons.

> ### S H O P T A L K
>
> Gamberg, Ruth, Winnifred Kwak, Meredith Hutchings and Judy Altheim with Gail Edwards. *Learning and Loving It: Theme Studies in the Classroom.* Portsmouth, New Hampshire: Heinemann, 1988.
>
>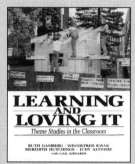
>
> After constructing a 7 x 5 foot playhouse on the playground, a class of six, seven, and eight year olds at the award-winning Dalhousie School in Nova Scotia turned enthusiastically to a theme cycle on "Houses of the World." They brainstormed research questions, researched using a variety of reference materials, and categorized and charted the information. After weeks of study, they constructed accurately detailed models. As a culmination of the study, the students held a learning fair and invited parents and friends. The young researchers displayed their models along with descriptive books and posters. They stood by their displays, explaining what they had learned to the interested visitors. This theme cycle, one of six which are described in inspiring detail, help readers understand the critical difference between a traditional thematic unit with "paste-on" activities and a core of the curriculum theme cycle from which flows multiple opportunities for authentic reading, writing, researching, and presenting. This is a book I wouldn't want to be without.

*Real learning is generative. One line of inquiry leads to another.*

Huntzinger began by reading aloud a variety of literature books all related to her theme of times past. The children discussed and made connections between the books and to their own experiences with their grandparents. They wrote letters to their grandparents and older friends and invited them to the classroom to share their favorite stories, childhood memories, and family artifacts. During the classroom visit, the children also interviewed and tape recorded each person, focusing specifically on what life was like when he or she was a child. How was life different? What machines did they use that are no longer used? How did language change? What slang words did they use that have vanished from our modern lexicon? With parent assistance, the stories the students captured on tape were transcribed, typed, illustrated, and published as a class book, "Stories from Long Ago."

As the children were coming to know the life stories of older adults they knew or who were affiliated with their classmates, they became sensitive to the elderly beyond their classroom door. Noticing a nursing home just down the street from their school, they wanted to know whether they could visit with the people there. With Huntzinger's assistance, they wrote a letter to the nursing home director and the result was a partner program that paired each kinder with an older friend. They took turns reading to each other and sharing holiday festivities. The children began to realize that many of their older friends were grappling with problems such as poor health, loneliness, and poverty stemming from fixed incomes.

The kindergartners' heightened sensitivity to problems faced by some elderly was challenged by an elderly homeless woman who pushed her shopping cart of belongings back and forth on the sidewalk outside of the school. Their questions and concern about her expanded their theme cycle in yet another direction, and led, eventually, to a stint working in a soup kitchen organized by the Sunnyvale Community Project for the Homeless. The children also sponsored car washes and bake sales and proudly donated the proceeds from their labor to the Project.

Real learning is generative. One line of inquiry leads to another. Adhering to state curriculum guidelines, Huntzinger chose to immerse her students in an exploration of aging and relationships. She provided a stimulating introduction to the topic through literature; but the children, engaged in the excitement of authentic learning, pushed the theme in directions Huntzinger had never even considered. One of the most exciting aspects of a theme cycle is that it enables children to investigate new lines of inquiry as they arise.

**Different Ways of Knowing.** The *Different Ways of Knowing* interdisciplinary curriculum created by the Galef Institute uses social studies themes as the focus of student inquiry across content areas and learning modalities. Students are invited to use the visual and performing arts, literature, writing, math, and science as learning tools to explore social studies themes. The structure is invitational—menu driven. Teachers and students map out their instructional pathways and adapt them along the way. Because learning is a nonlinear, recursive process of integrating prior knowledge with new knowledge, *Different Ways of Knowing* uses "wheels" as curriculum organizers for its four-phase learning model.

### Wheel 1: Exploring What You Already Know

Recognizing that children bring a great deal of knowledge to any learning event, teachers encourage students to explore and expand that knowledge. In Wheel 1, students are invited to discover and show what they already know about the theme or big idea of the module through drawing, dancing, writing, singing, pantomime, or other means of expression. *Different Ways of Knowing* helps teachers and students set a classroom climate for learning by valuing diversity of expression and expertise. All children participate and succeed, and their prior knowledge serves as a conceptual and motivational bridge to further exploration of the big idea of the module.

### Wheel 2: Getting Smarter Through Research

Compelling problems, guiding questions, and a classroom resource center full of diverse literature, reference books, and other media stimulate research in history and social studies, geography, economics, and other disciplines. Students work as partners, independent learners, and in groups exploring and interpreting what they read, see, and hear. They read stories, poetry, and nonfiction from many cultures and times. They learn through hands-on experiences and inquiry using maps, globes, photographs, artwork, and music. They conduct interviews and experiments, keep journals, and gather and analyze data; and "show what they know" in a wide variety of expressive forms. Self-assessment and reflection are a regular part of their learning.

### Wheel 3: Becoming an Expert

*Different Ways of Knowing* provides strategies and resources that support students as researchers. Building on their expanding knowledge, children focus their research, and work collaboratively. They pose their research questions, organize their group work, and, using both logical and intuitive skills, they share their findings with others in a variety of creative ways, such as radio dramas, journals, debate teams, murals, posters, dance, video newscasts, and so on. Their presentations demonstrate their understanding not only of the content but of the conventions and forms of verbal and nonverbal communication.

### Wheel 4: Making Connections to Lifelong Learning

Learning is a process of making connections, of understanding how things are related. As reflective learners, children connect what they're learning to their own lives. Thoughtful questions and learning events help children synthesize their new knowledge and apply it to new situations.

**S H O P T A L K**

Atwell, Nancie, ed. *Coming To Know: Writing To Learn in the Intermediate Grades.* Portsmouth, New Hampshire: Heinemann, 1989.

Anything written or edited by Nancie Atwell is well worth owning, and this book is no exception. Fourteen classroom teachers detail the strategies and materials they use to support their students' research across the curriculum. The book includes four valuable appendices: a list of different genres kids can use to publish their research, guiding questions for learning logs, lists of thematically related fiction and nonfiction books, and professional and commercial resources for both teachers and students that support reading and writing to learn.

## What About Skills?

As Ken Goodman (1986) reminds us, skills are easy to learn when we have a reason and need to learn them. Teachers in learner-centered classrooms often reserve direct instruction of specific skills for mini-lessons, a 7-10 minute lesson on a particular skill or strategy. The lesson is often in response to a student need that teachers have observed. For example, when students begin to play with dialogue in their written stories, they need to know about quotation marks. Mini-lessons enable teachers to help kids instructionally right at the point when they need information and assistance.

*Different Ways of Knowing* includes mini-lessons throughout each curriculum module, suggesting skills and strategies students may need at a given time to further their learning.

Mary Kitagawa uses mini-lessons to help her students refine their understanding of spelling and language mechanics. "For direct instruction on language mechanics and spelling," Kitagawa explains, "I reserve two half-hour periods a week, Monday and Friday, and I just teach whatever I think my students need. They write rules into a little booklet I have given them and sometimes we practice. This can be a spelling rule that I think they might find useful (the 1-1-1 rule that helps you know when to double the final consonant) or a punctuation rule (like putting quotation marks in dialogue). To make it a handwriting review, we also write all the rules in our booklets in cursive, and I go over difficult capital letters as I put the rule on the board.

I just found that there is so much to cover, and this way seems to be the most efficient. I find some carry over to their writing, and I can refer to the rule quickly in editing conferences without taking up much time."

Mini-lessons are most effective when they arise from a real need for skill or strategy work. As primary teacher Chris Boyd says, "I give mini-lessons as I see a need. Also, as children share things they are learning, opportunities for mini-lessons about a new skill or strategy become evident." And the final word on mini-lessons? Do keep them mini!

## Chapter 5

# Beyond the Classroom Door

It doesn't make good teaching sense to restrict children to the four walls of their classroom. A world of learning lies beyond the classroom door and extends into the community beyond the school. Let children out and let the community in. Here's how.

### Kids Helping Kids

We know the advantages of collaborative learning. But students can work with and help children in other classrooms as well. There are benefits for all when upper elementary students work with and tutor younger buddies in the primary grades. Alyce Dalzell in Peyton, Colorado, reports remarkable success with a Big Brother and Big Sister program that targets troubled older students. Upper elementary students who would like to participate are interviewed. Once the students are selected to serve as big brothers and sisters they must sign a contract with the homeroom teacher and the participating primary grade teacher. The students agree to follow specific mandatory behaviors: no gang clothes, no fighting, and they must complete their school work before they can visit their young friends. Big brothers and sisters participate in a training program in which they learn about positive expectations, desired dress code, acceptable language, and problem-solving strategies. As they work with their primary partners, big brothers and sisters experience success they may never have known before. The younger children seek them out on the playground and in the cafeteria to discuss problems or simply to share and spend time with them. It's an uplifting, helpful learning experience for both the younger and older students.

In Chris Boyd's kindergarten classroom, sixth graders visit every six days to read with their "kinder buddies." Boyd teaches them book-sharing techniques such as how to read with expression and how to ask the kinders open-ended questions about the stories. The older students also serve as kinder research partners. They read to the kinders a wide variety of both fiction and nonfiction materials. They also help the kinders take notes and, in general, help them keep track of what they are learning. When it comes time for the five year olds to share their research reports, the sixth graders help them rehearse. Using a microphone (to make it official!), the kinders give oral reports in addition to the written reports they publish as books or posters. With help from their older buddies, the whole research process becomes manageable for the five year olds.

*Older and younger students work well together and learn from each other.*

Sometimes older and younger children are paired to increase understanding among diverse groups. Mary Kitagawa reports that at her school, Marks Meadow in Amherst, Massachusetts, the orchestra teacher complained of rampant student put-downs. As a result, the staff decided to hold a "Civility Spring." They created multiage groupings of 15 kids from K–6, taking care to separate best friends. Every teacher or specialist met with a group once a week, engaging them in projects designed to help them form bonds. Kitagawa's group chose to learn Cat's Cradle string games. Other groups learned folk dances, painted murals, or learned to say and write welcome in many languages. A school night was set aside to celebrate. The school was opened to the community for group demonstrations. "It was so successful," Kitagawa recalls, "that we held a Civility Autumn when school began again the next year."

### Parents Count

In classroom learning communities, parents and family members are valued members. They are always welcome—not as sideline observers, but as active, contributing members of the classroom. My children attend Ohlone Elementary School in Palo Alto, California. At the beginning of the school year, all Ohlone parents receive a questionnaire. We're asked to list our interests, talents, and hobbies that we'd be willing to share with the students. The completed questionnaires are filed in the office. As kids across classrooms get involved with different projects, they can check the files to see if there is a school parent or family member who might know something about their chosen research topic. For instance, a friend of mine who worked as an archaeologist as a college student was recently interviewed by a group of sixth graders who were studying the archaeological ruins of Mesopotamia.

*Field Notes: Teacher-To-Teacher*

I send home letters at least monthly to keep parents informed of upcoming events, and to ask for their help in saving things for art, math, or cooking projects. Most of the parents work, but I constantly encourage them to stop by any time to see what we are doing. Many do, and a few volunteer to help out in the classroom. We have a foster grandmother, an elderly Navajo woman, who rotates through the classrooms and talks to the children in Navajo about traditional ways of doing things.

*Martha Ahlman*
*Chuska School*
*Tohatchi, New Mexico*

Chris Boyd sends out a survey, too, but says she's discovered that the "most effective way to find out about parent interests and expertise is to get to know them and to let them in on what we are studying. If they consistently know what's going on, they feel more confident about talking to me." Accordingly, Boyd sends home a newsletter every Monday. It has several sections.

- Concept Unit—explains to parents what the kinders are studying and why
- How To Help—suggests ways that parents can help their children at home
- Helpful Hints—gives nuts and bolts parenting tips
- Imagine—vignettes of authentic uses of reading and writing at home
- Parent Corner—acknowledges helpful parents, shares ideas from parents, and gives brief reviews of good books she's read or other parents have mentioned.

Don Howard teaches fifth grade in an inner city Chicago school. He understands that while working parents may not be able to take time off from their jobs to help inside the classroom, they still want to be involved. To meet their needs, he sends home a booklet entitled "Helping Outside the Classroom."

He outlines a variety of ways that parents can make significant classroom contributions on their own time at home.

- Bookbinding—making book covers for the stories students want to publish
- Making charts—parents are given large sheets of tagboard on which they can copy poems and songs in large print for all to see
- Attending field trips—chaperoning and helping the children learn from, enjoy, and share their field experience
- Arranging for guest speakers—arranging for different experts to come in and speak or demonstrate
- Fundraising—organizing money-making projects such as bake sales, book sales, car washes, garage sales, and so forth
- Word processing—typing up and preparing student compositions for publishing
- Collecting and constructing materials—helping to gather materials for math and art projects
- Carpentry—helping with a range of building projects
- Recording audiotapes of books—reading aloud stories on audiotape for the classroom listening center.

There are many ways to let parents know they are valued as educational partners. Every January, as the parent of three, I look forward to receiving the Ohlone School Parent-Student Questionnaire. It tells me that my children's teachers care about what my children and I think and feel regarding our Ohlone experiences. The teachers use the information to revise their instruction and curriculum, better meeting the needs and interests of parents and children.

## Ohlone School Parent-Student Questionnaire

- Please share this questionnaire with each child who attends Ohlone.
- Meet with him or her in a quiet place for twenty to thirty minutes.
- Read each question and discuss it together before answering it.
- In answering the questions, please keep in mind the academic, emotional, and social growth of your child this year.
- Return the questionnaire in an envelope to your child's classroom teacher.

**Student's name** _____

**Student's Grade Level:** K  1  2  3  4  5  (circle one)  **Teacher** _____

Keeping in mind the most useful responses are those which are specific, please fill out the following.

1.  Has the teacher been available to talk with you and been responsive to your concerns this year?

    Student's response _____

    Parent's response _____

2.  What is going well for you/your child this year?

    Student's response _____

    Parent's response _____

3.  In what ways do you feel you/your child is making progress?

    Student's response _____

    Parent's response _____

4.  What concerns (if any) do you have?

    Student's response _____

    Parent's response _____

5.  What suggestions do you have?

    Student's response _____

    Parent's response _____

6.  What questions do you have?

    Student's response _____

    Parent's response _____

7.  Please add any additional comments.

    Student's response _____

    Parent's response _____

Parent Signature(s) _____ Date_____

Student's Signature _____ Date_____

*Field Notes: Teacher-To-Teacher*

Every Thursday I look forward to the *Ohlone Arrow*, a weekly five-page plus school newsletter. Our principal, Michael Cass, shares schoolwide news or an inspirational tidbit in his weekly column, "Message from Michael." Upcoming field trips for every classroom are listed. The newsletter also features a biography and the photograph of one teacher or staff person. These biographical sketches help me get to know the many different people who serve the school and work with my children. Other features include reports from kids in different classrooms about the projects they are involved with. Parents who have helped in some way are acknowledged. There is even a baby column—new siblings are publicly welcomed into our Ohlone School community.

—LBB

Denise Ogren teaches kindergarten at Stinesville Elementary School in Stinesville, Indiana. Her kinders write many class books during the year. The first book is usually about their trip to the apple orchard. Each child writes about the trip and draws a picture on red paper shaped like an apple. Children read their messages to Ogren, and she types them up and helps the kids glue them on their apple pictures. The pages are glued back to front and then laminated and hooked together with metal rings. Children check the book out for the night. Ogren includes a message to the parents.

*Dear Readers:*

*This book is a result of our trip to the apple orchard. The children drew their own pictures and wrote their own words. Please take some time to read this with your child. Return this book tomorrow so other children can have a chance to take it home. We would like your comments about our book. Please add your words at the end.*

*Sincerely,*
*Denise Ogren*

Ogren explains the value of sending class-written books home: "Not only do parents see what we are doing at school, but they read the positive comments from other parents."

Susan Raedeke who teaches third grade in Crown Point, Indiana, invites parents to dialogue with her in a "Connections Notebook." Here is the letter she sends home to parents explaining the purpose of the Notebook.

*Dear Parents:*

*The purpose of this Connections Notebook is to connect learning that occurs in school with learning at home. The Notebook will allow us to become partners in your child's education.*

*This is how the Notebook will be used. At the end of each school day, we will review what took place and reflect on our learning. Then we will write something in the Notebook that might extend this learning at home. For example, your child might explain a new concept to you, ask you for your opinion or advice, discuss concerns from the classroom, or explain a school behavior problem.*

*Although this could be considered homework, participation is not required and the Notebook will not be graded. It is an invitation to be involved in your child's learning. You may become involved as little or as much as you wish.*

*1. Your child might ask you a question and then write your response in the Notebook.*

*2. You may write the response in the Notebook.*

*3. You may write to me if you have a concern about your child's learning.*

*4. Grandparents and other family members are welcome to participate.*

*Besides discussing our daily learning, I would also like to invite the third graders to read or be read to for about 20 minutes an evening. You or your child might want to write something in your Connections Notebook about what you have been reading or about how the reading is going.*

*Your child will bring the Notebook home each day, but I will understand if there are times when you cannot get to it. From time to time, I will keep the Notebook for an evening so that I can write to you. In this way, we can work together to help your child. I look forward to our year of learning together.*

*Cordially,*
*Susan Raedeke*

```
┌─────────────────────────────────────────────────────────────┐
│                     D I A L O G U E                           │
│                                                               │
│   How do I make parents feel welcome in my classroom?         │
│                                                               │
│   _____         │
│                                                               │
│   _____         │
│                                                               │
│                                                               │
│   What could I do to increase their participation?            │
│                                                               │
│   _____         │
│                                                               │
│   _____         │
│                                                               │
│                                                               │
│   How do I keep parents informed of what's happening?         │
│   ☐   weekly or monthly newsletters                           │
│                                                               │
│   ☐   parent potlucks or workshops                            │
│                                                               │
│   ☐   phone calls                                             │
│                                                               │
│   ☐   parent-teacher dialogue journals                        │
│                                                               │
│   ☐   other ways                                              │
│                                                               │
│                                                               │
│   _____         │
│                                                               │
│   _____         │
│                                                               │
└─────────────────────────────────────────────────────────────┘
```

*Learner-centered classrooms and schools are democratic communities of learners embedded within the culture and social experiences of the larger community.*

## The Larger Community

Learner-centered classrooms and schools are democratic communities of learners embedded within the culture and social experiences of the larger community. Luis Moll of the University of Arizona reminds educators that every community has "funds of knowledge," a pool of information, talents, and abilities that schools would do well to use. It makes good instructional and political sense for schools to tap funds available in their own communities.

I studied the Fair Oaks School in Redwood City, California (1989). This economically poor, barrio school has established a Community Resource Bank that lists the names, addresses, and phone numbers of local people who have expressed a willingness to share their knowledge, talents, and hobbies with Fair Oaks students. Students and teachers invite community experts into their classrooms for interviews or demonstrations. With adult supervision, students can also walk off the school grounds and interview the experts in their homes or work sites. In this way, students develop an appreciation for the rich learning possibilities and cultural heritage of their own communities. And community members appreciate the recognition they receive from the local public school. For all involved, there is a heightened awareness of our community and a new commitment to working together.

Fair Oaks Principal Craig Baker and his faculty have worked hard to make their school a viable part of the community. They've written and been awarded a number of private, local, and federal grants that have enabled them to design and implement several community programs.

**The after-school program.** Designed as after-school care for Fair Oaks students whose parents work, it has become a way to involve parents as teaching partners. Parents with special interests and talents are invited to teach classes which may last an afternoon, week, or month. One parent, for example, who is working on a nursing degree, taught a first aid class. With help from the San Mateo County Arts Council, the after-school program also includes a visual and performing arts component. The children have learned a variety of ethnic folk dances including Polynesian, Jamaican, and Mexican. Under the guidance of local artist Ramon Morales, the children have designed a mural which they will paint on the south wall of the school library.

**Parent literacy.** A federal grant entitled "Families as Learners and Teachers as Partners" has enabled the Fair Oaks community to create a Saturday Literacy Program for parents. Every Saturday from 11am to 1pm, parents attend classes on a variety of topics: ESL, literacy (many parents never had a chance to attend school themselves), and computer literacy. The grant pays for Gracelia Ybarra, a community member with experience as an adult education instructor.

## SHOPTALK

Taylor, Denny and Dorothy S. Strickland. *Family Storybook Reading.* Portsmouth, New Hampshire: Heinemann, 1986.

Katy Obringer, head librarian at Children's Library in Palo Alto, California says, "Taylor and Strickland provide telling accounts of parents sharing storybooks with their children. Through colorful vignettes of different families with varied lives, readers begin to see the critical connection between storybook reading and the acquisition of language and literacy. In addition to the informative real-life examples of reading aloud in the home, the authors give general guidelines for sharing stories and suggest specific books and activities."

**Raychem: A local partnership.** In addition to the ESL classes offered through the Saturday Literacy Program, a neighborhood business, Raychem, is sponsoring ESL classes for parents. These are held at night and include baby-sitting services for young children. Over the years, Raychem has given Fair Oaks several generous grants and Raychem employees are frequent visitors on the Fair Oaks campus, tutoring one-on-one, chatting with kids over lunch and, in general, providing academic and social support. (Check your own community for businesses or organizations that might be willing to adopt and sponsor your school.)

**Parent-Teacher Organization (PTO).** Parents and teachers also work together to raise funds for the school and to attend to a range of social and academic needs. Every spring and fall, they hold a *Kermese*, a festival that originated in Europe, but is also part of many Mexican communities. The Kermese features food, music (local bands donate their services), and games for the children. Last spring the festival earned $2,000 for Fair Oaks, money that can be used to purchase needed supplies, or pay for special services or field trips.

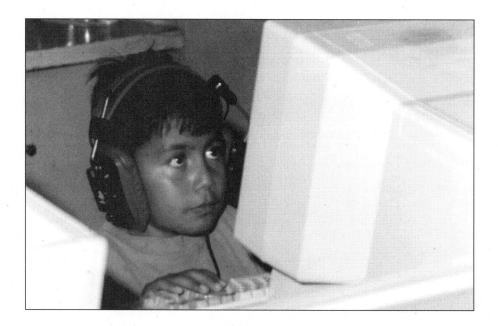

Anita Castaneda, a curriculum specialist, reports that the majority of the schools in the Fort Worth, Texas, School District have been adopted by a business, community, or civic organization. When a business adopts a school, they usually provide materials such as computer hardware and software, books, and funds for field trips; however, employees also may become personally involved in the school and serve as tutors, crossing guards, or playground supervisors. Tandy Corporation, one of the district's largest contributors, also provides generous scholarships for graduating high school seniors. Community and civic organizations provide a variety of services. Texas Wesleyan College contributes volunteer tutors and Christmas parties and gifts. Local nursing home residents are paired with middle school students. They write to each other, exchange gifts, and eat together at least twice a month. Officers from a police substation serve as crossing guards; they also read to students and eat with them so as to free the teachers during the lunch hour.

---

## DIALOGUE

How do I and my colleagues foster community involvement?

_____

_____

How might I involve local businesses or civic organizations in my school to work with students or to provide financial support?

_____

_____

How can I find out about grants available in my community on a state and federal level that might provide my school with much needed additional funds?

_____

_____

---

### The Pedagogy of Possibility

Classroom community is a theme that invites us to consider what education is really all about. What is the purpose of education? Why are we doing what we are doing, and what are we trying to accomplish? As I consider these questions, I am influenced by the work of my friend and colleague, Carole Edelsky, Professor of Education at Arizona State University. Edelsky has defined an educated person as one who has

- a questioning stance on life
- a passion for equality and justice
- extensive formal ways of knowing the world.

You'll discover a new sense of freedom as you create a classroom community in which both you and your students are able to explore questions and issues of personal interest and concern. But the liberating changes that we and our students experience will have no lasting impact unless we concern ourselves with greater social change. Critical pedagogists Paulo Freire, Henry Giroux, Michael Apple, and Patrick Shannon ask us to consider our role as educators beyond the classroom door. They ask us to consider the social and political implications of teaching and schooling. They ask us to work for change that will help *all* members of society realize the great promise of our democracy.

## SHOPTALK

Lewis, Barbara. *The Kid's Guide to Social Action: How To Solve the Social Problems You Choose—and Turn Creative Thinking Into Positive Action.* Minneapolis: Free Spirit Publishing, 1991.

Are you concerned about the pollution in your bay? Are you outraged that some children in this country go to bed hungry? Do you bemoan your city's restrictions on skateboarders? Get involved. Work for change. Make a difference. And for help every step of the way, read this book. Author and award-winning teacher Barbara Lewis gives detailed guides and tools for social action. With this book under your belt, you and your students will meet the challenge of the book's subtitle.

# Professional Bibliography

Apple, Michael. *Teachers and Texts: A Political Economy of Class and Gender Relations in Education.* New York: Routledge and Kegan Paul, 1986.

Atwell, Nancie. *In the Middle: Writing, Reading and Learning with Adolescents.* Portsmouth, New Hampshire: Heinemann, 1987.

Atwell, Nancie, ed. *Coming To Know: Writing To Learn in the Intermediate Grades.* Portsmouth, New Hampshire: Heinemann, 1989.

Barr, Mary. *The California Learning Record.* Sacramento: The California State Department of Education, 1993.

Baskwill, Jane and Paulette Whitman. *A Guide to Classroom Publishing.* New York: Scholastic, 1986.

Bridges, Lois. *Assessment: Continuous Learning.* Strategies for Teaching and Learning Professional Library, The Galef Institute. York, Maine: Stenhouse Publishers, 1995.

_____. *Writing as a Way of Knowing.* Strategies for Teaching and Learning Professional Library, The Galef Institute. York, Maine: Stenhouse Publishers (forthcoming).

Bridges Bird, Lois, ed. *Becoming a Whole Language School: The Fair Oaks Story.* Katonah, New York: Richard C. Owen, 1989.

Bridges Bird, Lois, Kenneth S. Goodman and Yetta M. Goodman, eds. *The Whole Language Catalog: Forms for Authentic Assessment*. New York: SRA: Macmillan/McGraw-Hill, 1994.

Buncombe, F. and Adrian Peetoom. *Literature-Based Learning: One School's Journey*. New York: Scholastic, 1988.

Calkins, Lucy. *The Art of Teaching Writing*. New Edition. Portsmouth, New Hampshire: Heinemann, 1994.

Calkins, Lucy and Shelly Harwayne. *Living Between the Lines*. Portsmouth, New Hampshire: Heinemann, 1990.

Crafton, Linda. *Whole Language: Getting Started...Moving Forward*. Katonah, New York: Richard C. Owen, 1991.

Cullinan, Bernice. *Children's Literature in the Reading Program*. Newark, Delaware: International Reading Association, 1987.

Donaldson, Margaret. *Children's Minds*. New York: Norton, 1978.

Duckworth, Eleanor. *The Having of Wonderful Ideas and Other Essays on Teaching and Learning*. New York: Teachers College Press, 1987.

Fisher, Bobbi. *Joyful Learning: A Whole Language Kindergarten*. Portsmouth, New Hampshire: Heinemann, 1991.

Freire, Paulo. *Pedagogy of the Oppressed*. New York: Seabury, 1970.

Gamberg, Ruth, Winifred Kwak, Meredith Hutchings and Judy Altheim with Gail Edwards. *Learning and Loving It: Theme Studies in the Classroom*. Portsmouth, New Hampshire: Heinemann, 1988.

Gardner, Howard. *Frames of Mind: The Theory of Multiple Intelligences*. New York: Basic Books, 1983.

Gee, Karolynne. *Visual Arts as a Way of Knowing*. Strategies for Teaching and Learning Professional Library, The Galef Institute. York, Maine: Stenhouse Publishers (forthcoming).

Gibbs, Jeanne. *Tribes*. Santa Rosa, California: Center Source Publications, 1987.

Giroux, Henry. *Teachers as Intellectuals: Toward a Critical Pedagogy of Learning*. Granby, Massachusetts: Bergin and Garvey, 1988.

Goodman, Kenneth S., Lois Bridges Bird and Yetta M. Goodman, eds. *The Whole Language Catalog*. New York: SRA: Macmillan/McGraw-Hill, 1991.

Goodman, Kenneth, Yetta Goodman and Wendy Hood. *The Whole Language Evaluation Book*. Portsmouth, New Hampshire: Heinemann, 1988.

Goodman, Kenneth. *What's Whole in Whole Language?* Portsmouth, New Hampshire: Heinemann, 1986.

Graves, Donald. *The Reading/Writing Teacher's Companion: Build a Literate Classroom.* Portsmouth, New Hampshire: Heinemann, 1991.

_____ . *Writing: Teachers and Children at Work.* Portsmouth, New Hampshire: Heinemann, 1983.

Harste, Jerome. "Inquiry-Based Instruction," *Primary Voices K-6,* April 1993.

Harste, Jerome, Kathy Short and Carolyn Burke. *Creating Classrooms for Authors.* Portsmouth, New Hampshire: Heinemann, 1985.

Harste, Jerome, Virginia Woodward and Carolyn Burke. *Language Stories and Literacy Lessons.* Portsmouth, New Hampshire: Heinemann, 1984.

Hart-Hewins, Linda and Jan Wells. *Borrow a Book: Your Classroom Library Goes Home.* New York: Scholastic, 1988.

Heller, Paul G. *Drama as a Way of Knowing.* Strategies for Teaching and Learning Professional Library, The Galef Institute. York, Maine: Stenhouse Publishers, 1995.

Hickman, Janet and Bernice Cullinan. *Children's Literature in the Classroom: Weaving Charlotte's Web.* Norwalk, Massachusetts: Christopher-Gordon, 1992.

Lamme, Linda, ed. *Learning To Love Literature.* Urbana, Illinois: National Council of Teachers of English, 1981.

Lewis, Barbara. *The Kid's Guide to Social Action: How To Solve the Social Problems You Choose—and Turn Creative Thinking into Positive Action.* Minneapolis: Free Spirit Publishing, 1991.

Manning, Deborah and Jean Fennacy. "Respect for Language and Learners in a Whole Language Classroom," *Whole Language: History, Philosophy and Practice,* edited by Sandra Brady and Toni Sills. Dubuque, Iowa: Kendall/Hunt Publishing Co., 1993.

McGuffee, Michael. "Hands-On Science," *The Whole Language Catalog,* edited by Kenneth S. Goodman, Lois Bridges Bird and Yetta M. Goodman. New York: SRA: Macmillan/McGraw-Hill, 1991.

Mersereau, Yvonne, Mary Glover and Meredith Cherland. "Dancing on the Edge," *The Whole Language Catalog,* edited by Kenneth S. Goodman, Lois Bridges Bird and Yetta M. Goodman. New York: SRA: Macmillan/ McGraw-Hill, 1991.

Mills, Heidi, David Whitin and Timothy O'Keefe. "Supporting Mathematical Understanding," *The Whole Language Catalog,* edited by Kenneth S.

Goodman, Lois Bridges Bird and Yetta M. Goodman. New York: SRA: Macmillan/McGraw-Hill, 1991.

Moss, Joy. *Focus on Literature: A Context for Literacy Learning.* Katonah, New York: Richard C. Owen, 1990.

National Academy Press. *Science for Children: Resources for Teachers.* Washington, DC: National Academy Press, 1990.

Nelsen, Jane. *Positive Discipline.* New York: Ballantine Books, 1987.

Ohanian, Susan. "There's Only One True Technique for Good Discipline," *Learning 82,* April 1982.

_____ .*Math as a Way of Knowing,* Strategies for Teaching and Learning Professional Library, The Galef Institute. York, Maine: Stenhouse Publishers, 1995.

Page, Nick. *Music as a Way of Knowing.* Strategies for Teaching and Learning Professional Library, The Galef Institute. York, Maine: Stenhouse Publishers, 1995.

Peterson, Ralph. *Life in a Crowded Place: Making a Learning Community.* Portsmouth, New Hampshire: Heinemann, 1992.

Poro, Barbara. "Tips on Helping Children Resolve Their Conflicts," received at a Parent Workshop at Ohlone Elementary School, Palo Alto, California, 1992.

Rudman, Marsha. *Children's Literature: Resource for the Classroom.* Norwood, Massachusetts: Christopher Gordon, 1991.

Shanon, Patrick. *Becoming Political.* Portsmouth, New Hampshire: Heinemann, 1992.

Short, Kathy. *Literature as a Way of Knowing.* Strategies for Teaching and Learning Professional Library, The Galef Institute. York, Maine: Stenhouse Publishers, (forthcoming).

Smith, Frank. "Twelve Easy Ways To Make Reading Difficult," *Essays into Literacy.* Portsmouth, New Hampshire, 1983.

Strickland, Dorothy. "The Child as Composer," *The Whole Language Catalog,* edited by Kenneth S. Goodman, Lois Bridges Bird and Yetta M. Goodman. New York: SRA: Macmillan/McGraw-Hill, 1991.

Taylor, Denny and Dorothy S. Strickland. *Family Storybook Reading.* Portsmouth, New Hampshire: Heinemann, 1986.

Watson, Dorothy, Carolyn Burke and Jerome Harste. *Whole Language: Inquiring Voices.* New York: Scholastic, 1989.

Weaver, Constance. *Understanding Whole Language: From Principles to Practice*. Portsmouth, New Hampshire: Heinemann, 1990.

Wells, Gordon. *The Meaning Makers: Children Learning Language and Using Language To Learn*. Portsmouth, New Hampshire: Heinemann, 1986.

Whitin, David, Heidi Mills and Timothy O'Keefe. *Living and Learning Mathematics: Stories and Strategies for Supporting Mathematical Literacy*. Portsmouth, New Hampshire: Heinemann, 1991.

Whitmore, Kathryn F. and Caryl G. Crowell. *Inventing a Classroom. Life in a Bilingual, Whole Language Learning Community*. York, Maine: Stenhouse Publishers, 1994.

# Professional Associations and Publications

The American Alliance for Health, Physical Education, Recreation, and Dance (AAHPERD)
*Journal of Physical Education, Recreation, and Dance*
1900 Association Drive
Reston, Virginia 22091

American Alliance for Theater and Education (AATE)
*AATE Newsletter*
c/o Arizona State University Theater Department
Box 873411
Tempe, Arizona 85287

American Association for the Advancement of Science (AAAS)
*Science Magazine*
1333 H Street NW
Washington, DC 20005

American Association of Colleges for Teacher Education (AACTE)
*AACTE Briefs*
1 DuPont Circle NW, Suite 610
Washington, DC 20036

American Association of School Administrators (AASA)
*The School Administrator*
1801 North Moore Street
Arlington, Virginia 22209

Association for Childhood Education International (ACEI)
*Childhood Education: Infancy Through Early Adolescence*
11141 Georgia Avenue, Suite 200
Wheaton, Maryland 20902

Association for Supervision and Curriculum Development (ASCD)
*Educational Leadership*
1250 North Pitt Street
Alexandria, Virginia 22314

The Council for Exceptional Children (CEC)
*Teaching Exceptional Children*
1920 Association Drive
Reston, Virginia 22091

Education Theater Association (ETA)
*Dramatics*
3368 Central Parkway
Cincinnati, Ohio 45225

International Reading Association
(IRA)
*The Reading Teacher*
800 Barksdale Road
Newark, Delaware 19714

Music Educators National Conference
(MENC)
*Music Educators Journal*
1806 Robert Fulton Drive
Reston, Virginia 22091

National Art Education Association
(NAEA)
*Art Education*
1916 Association Drive
Reston, Virginia 22091

National Association for the Education
of Young Children (NAEYC)
*Young Children*
1509 16th Street NW
Washington, DC 20036

National Association of Elementary
School Principals (NAESP)
*Communicator*
1615 Duke Street
Alexandria, Virginia 22314

National Center for Restructuring
Education, Schools, and Teaching
(NCREST)
*Resources for Restructuring*
P.O. Box 110
Teachers College, Columbia University
New York, New York 10027

National Council for the Social Studies
(NCSS)
*Social Education*
*Social Studies and the Young Learner*
3501 Newark Street NW
Washington, DC 20016

National Council of Supervisors of
Mathematics (NCSM)
*NCSM Newsletter Leadership in
Mathematics Education*
P.O. Box 10667
Golden, Colorado 80401

National Council of Teachers of
English (NCTE)
*Language Arts*
*Primary Voices K-6*
1111 Kenyon Road
Urbana, Illinois 61801

National Council of Teachers of
Mathematics (NCTM)
*Arithmetic Teacher*
*Teaching Children Mathematics*
1906 Association Drive
Reston, Virginia 22091

National Dance Association
(NDA)
*Spotlight on Dance*
1900 Association Drive
Reston, Virginia 22091

National Science Teachers Association
(NSTA)
*Science and Children*
*Science for Children: Resources for Teachers*
1840 Wilson Boulevard
Arlington, Virginia 22201

Phi Delta Kappa
*Phi Delta Kappan*
408 North Union
Bloomington, Indiana 47402

Society for Research in Music Education
*Journal for Research in Music Education*
c/o Music Educators National Conference
1806 Robert Fulton Drive
Reston, Virginia 22091

The Southern Poverty Law Center
*Teaching Tolerance*
400 Washington Avenue
Montgomery, Alabama 36104

Teachers of English to Speakers of Other
Languages (TESOL)
*TESOL Newsletter*
1600 Cameron Street, Suite 300
Alexandria, Virginia 22314

*Other titles in the*
*Strategies for Teaching and Learning Professional Library*

**Administrators** Supporting School Change
Robert Wortman
1-57110-047-4    paperback

In this fascinating personal account of how a principal can make a difference in the lives of all he touches through his work, noted principal Bob Wortman outlines his own strategies for creating a positive learning environment where everyone feels valued, respected, and can focus on the business of learning.

Fostering a successful school community demands more than a vision and a philosophy. A successful school administrator needs to know how to maintain positive relationships with all members of the school community—parents, students, and teachers. Classroom teachers, site and district administrators, parents, and policymakers will be interested in Bob's mission to create a schoolwide learning community that includes not only the people in the classrooms, but the support personnel, the families, and the community at large.

**Assessment** Continuous Learning
Lois Bridges
1-57110-048-2    paperback

Effective teaching begins with knowing your students, and assessment is a learning tool that enables you to know them. In this book Lois Bridges gives you a wide range of teacher-developed kidwatching and assessment forms to show different ways you can reflect on children's thinking and work. She offers developmental checklists, student and child interview suggestions, guidelines for using portfolios in your classroom, rubrics, and self-evaluation profiles. Also included are Dialogues that invite reflection, Shoptalks that offer lively reviews of the best and latest professional literature, and Teacher-To-Teacher Field Notes offering tips and experiences from practicing educators.

Lois identifies five perspectives on assessment—monitoring, observing, interacting, analyzing, and reporting—to think about when designing your own assessments. As you continuously evaluate and monitor your students' learning using a variety of assessment tools, you can design instruction and create curriculum that will stretch your students' knowledge and expand their learning worlds.

## **Drama** as a Way of Knowing
Paul G. Heller
1-57110-050-4    paperback

Paul Heller is an experienced teacher, playwright, and producer who is passionate about communicating through language, drama, and music. In this engaging book he shows you how to use drama as an effective part of all classroom learning. While making it clear you don't need previous dramatic training or experience, he presents the nuts and bolts of pantomime and improvisation, of writing and acting scenes, even creating and presenting large-scale productions.

Through his Ten-Step Process in which you, the teacher, are the director, he shows what you should do to guide your students through rewarding dramatic experiences. You will see that drama is a wonderful learning tool that enables students to explore multiple dimensions of their thinking and understanding. And not only is drama academically rewarding and beneficial, it's great fun as well!

## **Math** as a Way of Knowing
Susan Ohanian
1-57110-051-2    paperback

Award-winning author Susan Ohanian conducts a lively tour of classrooms around the country where "math time" means stimulating learning experiences. To demonstrate the point that mathematics is an active, ongoing way of perceiving and interacting with the world, she explores teaching mathematical concepts through hands-on activities; writing and talking about what numbers mean; discovering the where and why of math in everyday life; finding that there are often multiple ways to solve the same problem.

Focusing on the NCTM's *Curriculum and Evaluation Standards for School Mathematics*, Susan takes you into classrooms for a firsthand look at exciting ways the standards are implemented through innovative practices. She introduces you to new ways to organize your curriculum and classroom; suggests ways to create meaningful mathematics homework; gives you ideas to connect math across the curriculum; and links the reflective power of writing to support mathematical understanding.

For the nonspecialist in particular, Susan shows that math really is an exciting and powerful tool that students can really understand and apply in their lives.

**Music** as a Way of Knowing
Nick Page
1-57110-052-0    paperback

Nick Page loves to make and share music with his students, and it's likely that you will too by the time you've finished his passionate, thought-provoking book. You will also have developed a new understanding of and appreciation for the role music can play in supporting learners.

Rich with ideas on how to use music in the classroom, *Music as a Way of Knowing* will appeal especially to classroom teachers who are not musicians, but who enjoy and learn from music and want to use it with their students. Nick provides simple instructions for writing songs, using music to support learning across the curriculum, teaching singing effectively, and identifying good songs to use in the classroom.

He assures you that with time, all students can sing well. And once you've read this book, you'll have the confidence to trust yourself and your students to sing and learn well through the joy and power of music.